# PRACTICING
POSITIVE
LEADERSHIP

Other Books by Kim Cameron

Coffin Nails and Corporate Strategies (1982), with Robert H. Miles

Organizational Effectiveness: A Comparison of Multiple Models (1983), with David A. Whetten

Paradox and Transformation: Toward a Theory of Change in Organization and Management (1988), with Robert E. Quinn

Readings in Organizational Decline: Frameworks, Research, and Prescriptions (1988), with Robert I. Sutton and David A. Whetten

Positive Organizational Scholarship: Foundations of a New Discipline (2003), with Jane E. Dutton and Robert E. Quinn

Leading with Values: Positivity, Virtue, and High Performance (2006), with Edward D. Hess

Competing Values Leadership: Creating Value in Organizations (2006) with Robert E. Quinn, Jeff DeGraff, and Anjan V. Thakor

Making the Impossible Possible: Leading Extraordinary Performance—The Rocky Flats Story (2006), with Marc Lavine

The Virtuous Organization: Insights from Some of the World's Leading Management Thinkers (2008), with Charles C. Manz, Karen P. Manz, and Robert D. Marx

Developing Management Skills, 8th ed. (2011), with David A. Whetten

Organizational Effectiveness (2010)

Diagnosing and Changing Organizational Culture: Based on the Competing Values Framework, 3rd ed. (2011), with Robert E. Quinn

The Oxford Handbook of Positive Organizational Scholarship (2012), with Gretchen M. Spreitzer

Positive Leadership: Strategies for Extraordinary Performance, 2nd ed. (2012)

PRACTICING POSITIVE LEADERSHIP

TOOLS AND TECHNIQUES THAT CREATE EXTRAORDINARY RESULTS

KIM CAMERON

BK

Berrett–Koehler Publishers, Inc.
San Francisco
a BK Business book

Berrett-Koehler Publishers, Inc.
235 Montgomery Street, Suite 650
San Francisco, CA 94104-2916
Tel: (415) 288-0260   Fax: (415) 362-2512   www.bkconnection.com

Ordering Information

Quantity sales. Special discounts are available on quantity purchases by corporations, associations, and others. For details, contact the "Special Sales Department" at the Berrett-Koehler address above.

Individual sales. Berrett-Koehler publications are available through most bookstores. They can also be ordered directly from Berrett-Koehler: Tel: (800) 929-2929; Fax: (802) 864-7626; www.bkconnection.com

Orders for college textbook/course adoption use. Please contact Berrett-Koehler: Tel: (800) 929-2929; Fax: (802) 864-7626.

Orders by U.S. trade bookstores and wholesalers. Please contact Ingram Publisher Services, Tel: (800) 509-4887; Fax: (800) 838-1149; Email: customer.service@ingrampublisherservices.com; or visit www.ingram publisherservices.com/Ordering for details about electronic ordering.

Berrett-Koehler and the BK logo are registered trademarks of Berrett-Koehler Publishers, Inc.

Printed in the United States of America

Berrett-Koehler books are printed on long-lasting acid-free paper. When it is available, we choose paper that has been manufactured by environmentally responsible processes. These may include using trees grown in sustainable forests, incorporating recycled paper, minimizing chlorine in bleaching, or recycling the energy produced at the paper mill.

Library of Congress Cataloging-in-Publication Data

Cameron, Kim S.
    Practicing positive leadership : tools and techniques that create extraordinary results / Kim Cameron. — First edition.
        pages cm
    Includes bibliographical references and index.
    ISBN 978-1-60994-972-3 (pbk. : alk. paper) 1. Leadership. I. Title.
    HD57.7.C3546 2013
    658.4'092—dc23
                                                                    2013025988

First Edition

18 17 16 15 14 13   10 9 8 7 6 5 4 3 2 1

Cover design: Crowfoot Design/Leslie Waltzer

This book is dedicated to the many inspiring leaders in my life who have demonstrated extraordinary courage, insight, and wisdom in their applications of positive leadership practices. I have been fortunate to observe many individual and organizational transformations as a result of positive leadership in businesses, educational institutions, the United States military, the national intelligence agencies, health care organizations, and church service. The positive leaders who have inspired me are too many to enumerate, but I am indebted to them all.

I also dedicate this book to my wife, Melinda, the mother of our seven children and grandmother to, so far, eighteen and a half grandchildren. She is the best example of practicing positive leadership that I have ever known.

☀ CONTENTS

 # PREFACE

This book was motivated by feedback from a variety of colleagues and respected leaders who wanted to see more information on putting the strategies of positive leadership into practice. In an earlier book, *Positive Leadership*, I identified four key strategies that have been shown to produce extraordinarily positive performance in organizations. These strategies include the creation of a *positive climate, positive relationships, positive communication*, and *positive meaning*. Substantial empirical evidence from a wide variety of organizations confirms that these strategies are crucial for achieving what I call "positively deviant" levels of performance—that is, performance that allows individuals and organizations to achieve their highest potential, flourish at work, experience elevating energy, and achieve levels of effectiveness difficult to attain otherwise.

This book offers five sets of very concrete positive leadership practices to help leaders implement the four positive strategies in all types of organizations, including businesses, educational institutions, health care organizations, community associations, sports teams, and families. Organizational change agents—whether internal or external consultants, unit leaders, or parents—will find this book to be of particular relevance.

Specifically, the book addresses the criticisms of some detractors that positive leadership is too soft, touchy-feely, smiley-face, saccharine, New Age, or naive. Some claim that positive leadership ignores the hard-nosed, competitive, and challenging aspects of leadership. While the positive practices outlined in this book are aimed at producing positive results, they are not synonymous with mere sweetness or indulgence. They are intended to help leaders address common challenges and difficult obstacles that characterize all organizational settings. Positive leadership practices are anything but superficial and permissive. They require effort and tenacity if positively deviant results are to be produced.

The practices described in the book have been selected because they are less well known than common organizational intervention techniques such as team building, trust building, consensus building, and influence building. The practices here are meant to supplement those useful common techniques. They have been tested in the field as well as having their credibility confirmed in scientific research. Though not all of the practices will be applicable in all organizational settings, you are likely to find several that will assist you in achieving extraordinarily positive performance.

I owe a debt of gratitude to many of my colleagues who have provided insight into the practices associated with positive leadership and who have served as role models for putting them into action. I am especially grateful to my faculty colleagues in the Center for Positive Organizational Scholarship at the University of Michigan: Wayne Baker, Jane Dutton, Shirli Kopelman, David Mayer, Carlos Mora, Robert Quinn, Gretchen Spreitzer, and Lynn Wooten. The staff at Berrett-Koehler deserves accolades for being the best publisher on the planet; special thanks go to Steven Piersanti and Jeevan Sivasubramaniam. External reviewers Tom Kruse, Jackie Stavros, and Leigh Wilkinson offered very helpful suggestions for improvements in the manuscript. Colleagues in the Ross School of Business Executive Education Center have provided many opportunities to interact with organizations as well as valuable feedback; special thanks are due to Melanie Barnett, Cheri Alexander, and the outstanding staff. Especially, my assistant, Meredith Smith, has made this work possible through extraordinary support, organization, and encouragement. Thank you very much to all.

1
WHY PRACTICE POSITIVE LEADERSHIP?

The University of Michigan's Ross School of Business recently announced a new strategic plan to guide business education through the next decade and beyond. A key strategic pillar is an emphasis on the positive—positive business, positive leadership, and making a positive difference in the world.

Humana, one of the largest health insurance providers in the United States, recently changed its identity from being an insurance company to being a well-being company. The primary objective is to create benefits for employees and customers by implementing practices based on positive leadership and positive organizational scholarship.

Toshi Harada, Director of International Business Development at Hayes Lemmertz—the world's largest producer of automobile wheels—equates positive leadership with Japanese manufacturing principles. "A signature feature of Japanese manufacturing philosophy is the elimination of waste. Negative leaders represent waste and inefficiency," he suggests, "whereas positive leadership produces sustainable improvement."[1]

Jim Mallozzi, former CEO of one of the Prudential Financial Services businesses, turned around the financial performance in his organization by providing his top team "the latitude to experiment on being positively deviant leaders." Financial results changed in one year from a $140 million loss to a $20 million profit through applying practices of positive leadership.[2]

George Mason University has recently engaged in an institution-wide effort to become the world's first well-being university by, among other things, integrating positive leadership practices throughout the entire system. Both top-down and bottom-up interventions are being initiated.

Producing extraordinarily high performance, generating positively deviant results, and creating remarkable vitality in the workplace are the primary objectives of positive leadership. Positive leadership involves the implementation of multiple positive practices that help individuals and organizations achieve their highest potential, flourish at work, experience elevating energy, and reach levels of effectiveness difficult to attain otherwise. The practices included in this book can help produce such extraordinarily positive results.

Empirical research by recent scholars, as well as anecdotal evidence such as the examples described above, confirms that positive leadership practices produce results that exceed normal or expected performance. And while the evidence that positive leadership brings improvement in *organizational* productivity, profitability, quality, innovation, and customer loyalty might not be unexpected, many may be surprised to learn that there is published evidence that this revolutionary approach to leading and managing produces benefits in terms of *individual* physiological health, emotional well-being, brain functioning, interpersonal relationships, and learning as well.[3]

Lingering questions have been raised regarding positive leadership, such as: Exactly how are these results achieved? What tools or techniques can managers implement to obtain positive results in their organizations? What specifically can leaders do to practice positive leadership? This book will show you. It builds on and supplements my previous book *Positive Leadership*. That earlier work provided evidence showing how four positive leadership strategies—that create a positive climate, positive relationships, positive communication, and positive meaning—can produce exceptional results.

Here I present specific practices and activities that can serve as guides for implementing those four positive leadership strategies. As Figure 1 shows, each of the practices (in the box corners) interacts with more than one of the leadership strategies (in darker-colored ovals). The figure illustrates the relationships among the positive leadership practices presented in this book and the four strategies in the *Positive Leadership* book.

Throughout the book I will summarize empirical research that has established the validity of the practices and discuss how real organizations have successfully applied them to produce positive results.[4] Activities are

FIGURE 1

Relationships Between Positive Leadership Practices and Positive Strategies

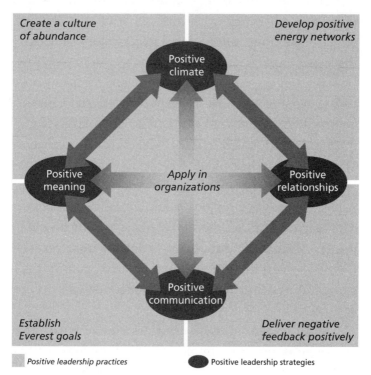

provided in each chapter so that you can immediately implement the practices in your own organizations.

POSITIVE LEADERSHIP IS HELIOTROPIC

Practicing positive leadership is important because positivity is heliotropic. That is, all living systems have a tendency to move toward positive energy and away from negative energy, or toward what is life-giving and away from what is life-depleting.[5] One form in which we experience positive energy in nature is sunlight. In human interactions, it often takes the form of interpersonal kindness and gratitude. Positive leadership practices engender positive energy and unlock resources in people because, like all biological systems, human beings possess inherent inclinations toward the positive.

You can see examples of the heliotropic effect in both individuals and organizations.[6] For instance, people are more accurate in processing positive information—whether the task involves verbal discrimination, organizational behavior, or judging emotion—than negative information. People reported thinking about positive statements 20 percent longer than negative statements and almost 50 percent longer than neutral statements, and positive information can be recalled more easily and more accurately than negative information. People more effectively learn and remember positive terms and events than neutral or negative ones: when presented with lists of positive, neutral, and negative words, for example, people are more accurate in recalling the positive, and the longer the delay between learning and recalling, the more positive bias is displayed. Managers are much more accurate in rating subordinates' competencies and proficiencies when the subordinates perform correctly than when they perform incorrectly.

We tend to seek out positive stimuli and avoid negative stimuli, as evidenced by people's judgments that from two-thirds to three-quarters of the events in their lives are positive. Further, most people say they are positive, optimistic, and happy most of the time. Positive words have higher frequencies in all the languages that have been studied to date, and positive words typically entered English usage more than 150 years before their negative opposites (for example, "better" entered before "worse"). Central nervous system functioning (i.e., vagus nerve health) is most effective, the density of the brain's gray matter is enhanced, and coherence of bodily rhythms is at its peak when people experience positive and virtuous conditions compared to neutral or negative conditions.[7]

Several studies have highlighted how being exposed to positive influences increases life expectancy. Pressman and Cohen, for example, examined the journals of famous psychologists of the past and counted the positive and negative words used in their writing. Psychologists whose writings used a greater number of positive words lived an average of six to seven years longer than their more negative colleagues.[8] Pressman also studied famous singers and found that those who sang love songs with positive words lived an average of fourteen years longer than those who sang love songs with angry words. (Interestingly, the content of the song did not affect the life expectancy of the person who wrote the song, only that of the person who repeatedly sang the song.)[9] Snowden's well-known study of 678 Catholic nuns also found that those using the greatest number of positive words in their journals and autobiographical essays when they entered the convent lived an average of twelve years longer than their counterparts.[10] A bias toward the positive, in other words, characterizes human beings in their thoughts, judgments, emotions, language, interactions, and physiological functioning. It is natural for humans to incline toward the positive, and empirical evidence suggests that positivity is the preferred and natural state of human beings, just as it is among other biological systems. Positive leadership practices promote a heliotropic effect, helping people to move toward the positive.

YEAH, BUT NEGATIVE DOMINATES POSITIVE

On the other hand, a great deal of evidence also exists that human beings react more strongly to the negative than to the positive.[11] Negative news sells more newspapers than positive news, people pay more attention to critical comments than to compliments, and traumatic events have greater impact than positive ones. All living systems react strongly and quickly to threats to their existence or signals of maladaptation.

For example, the effects of negative information and negative events take longer to wear off than the effects of positive information or pleasant events. A single traumatic experience (e.g., abuse, violence) can overcome the effects of many positive events, but a single positive event does not usually overcome the effects of even a single traumatic event. A positive event is remembered more accurately and longer, but a negative event has more effect on immediate memory and salience in the short run. Negative events have a greater effect on people's subsequent moods and adjustments than positive events, and negative or upsetting social interactions weigh more heavily on people than positive or helpful interactions, often producing depression or bad moods. People tend to spend more time thinking about threatening personal relationships than about supportive ones, and about personal goals that were blocked compared to those that were not blocked. When negative things happen (for example, people lose a wager, endure abuse, or become a victim of a crime), they spend more time trying to explain the outcome or to make sense of it than when a positive outcome occurs.

In human interactions, undesirable human traits receive more weight in impression formation than desirable traits. Bad reputations are easy to acquire but difficult to lose, whereas good reputations are difficult to acquire but easy to lose. In initial hiring decisions, 3.8 unfavorable bits of information are required to shift an initial positive decision to rejection, whereas 8.8 favorable pieces of information are necessary to shift an initial negative decision to acceptance. To be categorized as good, for example, one has to be good all the time, but to be categorized as bad, one only has to engage in a few bad acts.

> Events that are negatively valenced (e.g., losing money, being abandoned by friends, and receiving criticism)

will have a greater impact on the individual than positively valenced events of the same type (e.g., winning money, gaining friends, and receiving praise). This is not to say that bad will always triumph over good, spelling doom and misery to the human race. Rather, good may prevail over bad by superior force of numbers: Many good events can overcome the psychological effects of a single bad one. When equal measures of good and bad are present, however, the psychological effects of bad ones outweigh those of the good ones.[12]

An important function of positive leadership, therefore, is to demonstrate tools, techniques, and practices that can overcome the effects of the negative. When positive practices are given greater emphasis than negative practices, individuals and organizations tend to flourish.

POSITIVE LEADERSHIP AND ORGANIZATIONAL PERFORMANCE

Individual effects are not the same as organizational effects, of course. In organizations, leaders must address multiple constituencies. Processes, routines, and structures must be considered. Cultures, embedded values, and traditions must be respected. Employee preferences and relationships must be taken into account. An important question, therefore, is whether positive practices produce positive outcomes in organizations as they do in individuals.

In the last decade, substantial empirical evidence has demonstrated that positive leadership practices produce good outcomes in organizations, just as positivity does with individuals. Studies in several industries and sectors have shown, for example, that organizations that implemented positive practices increased their profitability, productivity, quality, customer satisfaction, and employee retention.[13]

One early study, for example, assessed positive practices and outcomes in seven organizations in the transportation industry. The results (shown in Figure 2) suggest that the greater the positive practices in these firms, the higher the organizational performance on six dimensions—profitability, productivity, quality, innovation, customer satisfaction, and employee retention. This study was then expanded to include organizations across sixteen different industries and included both for-profit and not-for-profit organizations. The organizations studied encompassed both large firms such as General Electric, National City Bank, and OfficeMax as well as small and not-for-profit firms such as the YMCA, hospitals, and educational organizations. The results matched those in Figure 2: organizations that implemented positive practices were significantly more effective than organizations that did not.

Another investigation was conducted in the U.S. airline industry following the tragedy of September 11, 2001. After the World Trade Center towers came down and the Pentagon was attacked, all flights were suspended for several days. When the airlines were allowed to fly passengers again, ridership topped out at 80 percent of previous ridership levels. The problem is, the economic

FIGURE 2

Firm Performance and Positive Leadership Practices

Source: Cameron, Bright, and Caza, 2004.

model of the U.S. airline industry was based on an 86 percent seat-fill rate, so all of the airlines had substantial excess capacity and costs. Figure 3 shows the amount of downsizing implemented by each company.

Each airline approached downsizing and cost cutting in a different way. Some approaches were more consistent with positive leadership practices than others For example, US Airways responded by downsizing more than 20 percent and by declaring financial exigency, which meant that it could lay off employees with no benefits and no severance and that union contracts were rendered null and void. Southwest Airlines, on the other

FIGURE 3

Relationship Between Downsizing by U.S. Airline Companies after 9-11 and Financial Return September 2001–2002

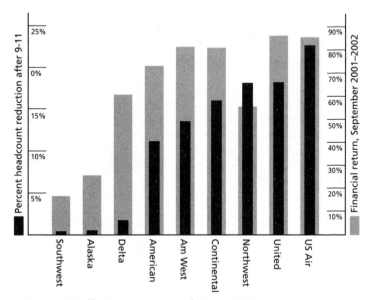

Source: Gittell, Cameron, Lim, and Rivas, 2006.

hand, laid off no one: "You want to show your people that you value them, and that you aren't going to hurt them just to get a little more money in the short run. Not furloughing people breeds loyalty. It breeds a sense of security. It breeds a sense of trust."[14]

The problem is that failing to reduce the number of employees and lower the associated costs can put the airline company's viability at risk. Stockholders and investors are impervious to how employees are treated. Wall Street has just one goal: provide a return on investment. This might suggest that Southwest Airlines would be punished severely by Wall Street investors for its refusal to cut jobs.

Nine airline companies were distinguished in terms of the extent to which they followed practices of positive leadership in their approach to downsizing. Some did so in a way that preserved the dignity, financial support, and safety nets of employees, while others did not. As illustrated in Figure 3, the correlation between stock price or financial return to these companies in the following twelve months and the extent to which they consistently utilized positive leadership practices is .86. Firms that implemented positive leadership practices made significantly more money and recovered more quickly than those that did not.[15]

Two additional studies—one investigating forty financial services organizations and one looking at thirty health care organizations—produced similar results. In those studies, performance improvements over a multi-year period were examined to determine the relationship between positive leadership and organizational performance. Positive leadership practices were measured over a two-year period, and then a year later performance was measured. In both industries, when positive leadership practices were implemented, performance scores also improved significantly. Figure 4 shows the health care organizations' outcomes after positive leadership practices were implemented: double-digit improvement occurred on a variety of performance dimensions.[16]

These studies clearly show that positive leadership practices can produce significant improvement in all

FIGURE 4

Percent Improvement in Health Care Over Two Years

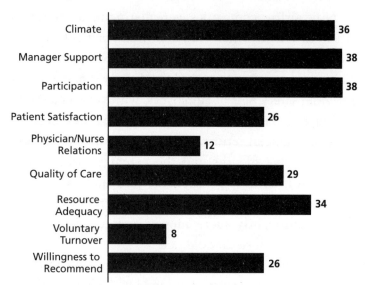

Climate	36
Manager Support	38
Participation	38
Patient Satisfaction	26
Physician/Nurse Relations	12
Quality of Care	29
Resource Adequacy	34
Voluntary Turnover	8
Willingness to Recommend	26

Source: Cameron, Mora, Leutscher, and Calarco, 2011.

types of organizations. The practices introduced in this book have been implemented in organizations across several industries, including health care, the military, government, education, financial services, manufacturing, and retail. Their usefulness is not limited to a particular sector or type of organization.

POSITIVE LEADERSHIP PRACTICES, TOOLS, AND TECHNIQUES

Chapter 2, "How to Create a Culture of Abundance," details five specific steps aimed at organizational culture change. The first step focuses on creating readiness for culture change—for example, by identifying standards for comparison and by altering language and symbols. All change is accompanied by resistance, so the second step discusses tools and techniques for overcoming resistance. When readiness has been created and resistance reduced, people need to know what the new culture will be like, so the third step involves articulating a vision of abundance. A vision of abundance always contains both left brain and right brain attributes. The fourth step features activities that will generate commitment to the vision and to the new culture. Commitment and participation are highly related. The fifth step, fostering sustainability, ensures that the culture of abundance will become institutionalized and can be sustained over time.

It is almost impossible to be a positive leader without also being a source of positive energy. Therefore, Chapter 3, "How to Develop Positive Energy Networks," summarizes the evidence showing that positively energizing leaders create remarkable performance in other people and in their organizations. The chapter also provides several specific tools and techniques for developing positive energy that have been successfully applied in a variety of settings. These include practices associated with recreational work, contribution activities, and mapping energy networks.

Positive leadership does not mean constant smiling and sweet interactions. Sometimes positive leaders must deliver negative messages, address problems, or tackle difficult issues. Chapter 4, "How to Deliver Negative

Feedback Positively," guides leaders through a series of tools, techniques, and practices that help build and strengthen relationships even though corrective or disapproving feedback must be delivered. Practices for being critical without producing defensiveness, bruising egos, or invalidating opposing points of view are highlighted.

Goal setting is a very common technique for motivating performance and for maintaining accountability. Chapter 5, "How to Establish and Achieve Everest Goals," highlights the differences between normal goal setting and identifying Everest goals. Everest goals possess the same attributes as the better-known SMART goals—both types are specific, measurable, aligned, realistic, and time-bound—but Everest goals possess five additional attributes that make them unique. They are associated with positive deviance—extraordinarily positive and even virtuous performance; they are associated with inherent value; they possess an affirmative orientation rather than a problem-solving orientation; they aim to provide a contribution regardless of personal benefit; and they create and foster sustainable positive energy. This chapter provides ways to identify and work toward the achievement of both individual and organizational Everest goals.

Positive leadership most often occurs in the context of an organization, and what works in interpersonal interactions may not necessarily work the same way in organizational contexts. Organizational dynamics frequently introduce complexities, competing values, and the need for trade-offs. In Chapter 6, "How to Apply Positive Leadership in Organizations," the Competing Values Framework is briefly introduced and is used to demonstrate different types of tools and techniques for implementing positive leadership in organizational settings. The criticism that positive leadership emphasizes kindness and gentleness at the expense of the hard-nosed, competitive, challenging aspects of leadership is countered in this chapter. Tools and practices are introduced that address both the soft and the hard side of leadership.

CONCLUSION

This book provides a variety of tools, techniques, and practices that supplement rather than duplicate the more commonly prescribed self-help prescriptions. The practices described here all meet three criteria: they have been confirmed by valid empirical research, they are grounded in theory, and they have been applied in a range of organizational settings. Each practice has helped positive leaders produce extraordinarily positive results in organizations—and can help you produce positive results in yours.

2
HOW TO CREATE
A CULTURE OF ABUNDANCE

Organizational culture is one of the most important predictors of high levels of performance over time.[1]
Organizations that flourish have developed a *culture of
abundance*, which builds the collective capabilities of
all members. It is characterized by the presence of numerous positive energizers throughout the system, including embedded virtuous practices, adaptive learning,
meaningfulness and profound purpose, engaged members, and positive leadership. There is plenty of empirical
evidence that organizations displaying a culture of abundance have significantly higher levels of performance
than others.[2] Since creating a culture of abundance almost always implies culture change, this chapter discusses five basic steps that positive leaders can use to
facilitate such a change: creating readiness for change,
overcoming resistance to change, articulating a vision of
abundance, generating commitment to that vision, and
making the new culture sustainable over time.

WHAT IS ORGANIZATIONAL CULTURE?

When we speak of an organization's culture, we are referring to the taken-for-granted values, expectations, collective memories, and implicit meanings that define that organization's core identity and behavior. Culture reflects the prevailing ideology that people carry inside their heads. It provides unwritten and usually unspoken guidelines for what is acceptable and what is not. Culture is largely invisible until it is challenged or contradicted. We do not wake up each morning, for example, making a conscious choice to speak our dominant language—in my case, English. We are not aware that we speak a certain language until we meet someone who does not, calling our attention to what we take for granted. And because culture is undetectable most of the time, it is difficult to manage or change.

At the most fundamental level, culture can be characterized as the implicit assumptions that define the human condition and its relationship to the environment. Figure 5 illustrates the different levels and manifestations of culture, from the taken-for-granted and unobservable elements to the more overt and noticeable elements.

At the very foundation of culture lies human virtues—what all human beings consider to be right and good, and what allows human beings to be their very best. These are *implicit assumptions*. Freedom, justice, compassion, kindness, faith, charity, courage, and love are among the attributes that all human beings assume to be right and

FIGURE 5

Organizational Culture

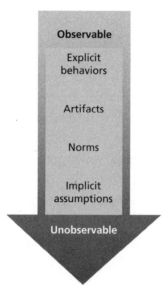

good. Implicit assumptions and values give rise to social contracts and *norms*. These are the conventions and procedures that govern how humans interact—including rules of etiquette, civility, and courtesy. *Artifacts* are manifestations of culture that are more observable and overt, such as the buildings in which we live, the clothes we wear, the entertainment we enjoy, and the logos, flags, graffiti, and decorations we use to identify ourselves. The most obvious manifestation of culture is the *explicit behavior* of members of the culture. In a group or organization, this is the way in which people interact, the language that is expected, or the ways in which relationships are formed.

When leaders attempt to foster a change in culture, they usually begin by encouraging change in overt behaviors and observable features. By themselves, these kinds of changes do not signal a cultural shift, but they begin the process of deeper and more fundamental culture change. The challenge for positive leaders is to ensure that these initial efforts to establish abundance become embedded and institutionalized, so that culture change actually occurs. The sustainability of abundance is the goal. A quote from Mahatma Gandhi describes this process: "Keep your thoughts positive, because your thoughts become your words. Keep your words positive, because your words become your behavior. Keep your behavior positive, because your behavior becomes your habits. Keep your habits positive, because your habits become your values. Keep your values positive, because your values become your destiny."[3]

Positive leaders know that a culture change has occurred when members of the organization begin to think in new ways, change their paradigms or the categories they use to make sense of their environments, alter the meaning associated with their activities, focus on possibilities instead of just probabilities, and experience a change in ideology.

AN EXAMPLE OF CULTURE CHANGE: GENERAL MOTORS

In the 1980s General Motors built a production facility in Fremont, California, where the Chevrolet Nova automobile was assembled. The plant operated at a disastrously low level of productivity. Absenteeism averaged 20 percent, and approximately five thousand grievances were filed each year by employees at the plant—the same as the total number of workers. Three or four times each year, workers just walked off the job in wildcat strikes. Sales were trending downward, and ratings of quality, productivity, and customer satisfaction were the worst in the company. Because of this disastrous performance, GM shuttered the plant and laid off all the workers.

Then, in the interest of trying to create a culture change, General Motors approached Toyota to design and build a car as a joint venture. Toyota jumped at the chance to work with what was at the time the world's largest auto company. The Fremont facility was selected as the site for this joint venture, and approximately eighteen months after being idled, the plant was reopened. Two years after the restart of operations, absenteeism was 2 percent, no strikes had occurred, and sales, productivity, quality, and customer satisfaction were the highest in General Motors.

One of the production employees who had worked at the plant for more than twenty years, both under the old regime and then in the new joint venture, was asked to describe the changes that occurred after Toyota and General Motors joined forces. Before the plant was closed, employees felt they had no real stake in the organization; consequently, many of them would deliberately think up ways to mess up the system. This employee would leave part of his sandwich behind the door panel of a car, for example. A month later, the customer who bought the car would notice a terrible smell but not be able to figure out where it was coming from. Or he would put loose screws in a compartment of the frame that was to be welded shut so that the rattle could be heard throughout the entire frame of the car.

After the plant reopened under the joint venture, a new company culture was created in which employees were encouraged to adopt positive ways of thinking about the company and their role in it. For example, each employee was allowed to choose his or her job title. This worker, whose job was to monitor robots that spot-welded parts of the frame together, selected the title, "Director of Welding Improvement." All employees were given business cards with their new title as a symbol of a new culture of abundance. One result was a dramatic change in the sense of ownership and engagement: "Now when I go to a San Francisco 49ers game or a Golden State Warriors game or a shopping mall," this worker said, "I look for our cars in the parking lot. When I see one, I take out my business card and write on the back of it, 'I made your car. Any problems, call me.' I put my card under the windshield wiper. I do it because I feel personally responsible for those cars."[4]

This example illustrates a fundamental culture change—a gut-level, values-centered, in-the-bones change in what is assumed to be right and acceptable. Employees adopted a different way to think about the company and their roles in it, with the result that productivity, quality, efficiency, and morale improved significantly. Ample empirical evidence confirms that an abundance culture and virtuous practices in organizations lead to dramatic positive impacts on performance and effectiveness.[5]

In the rest of this chapter you will find a series of practical steps shown in Figure 6 for developing a culture

FIGURE 6

Creating a Culture of Abundance

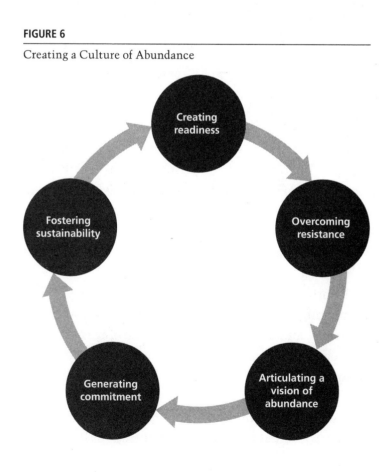

of abundance: creating readiness, overcoming resistance, articulating a vision of abundance, generating commitment, and fostering sustainability. It is important to stress that each of the steps is necessary—each relies on and reinforces the ones that come before. This means that if any one step is skipped, culture change will not occur. It is also essential to note that although these steps stimulate the process of culture change, they do not guarantee it. Culture change takes time and persistence, but applying these steps is a proven way to produce a culture of abundance.

CREATING READINESS

One way to create readiness for culture change is to compare current levels of performance to the highest standards you can find. Identifying who else performs at spectacular levels, studying those best practices in detail, and then identifying ways to exceed them permits you to set a standard toward which people can aspire. It identifies a target of opportunity.

Identifying best practices does not mean copying or mimicking. Rather, it means capturing new information, new ideas, and new perspectives and learning from them.

Here are several kinds of standards you can use for comparison.

Comparative standards: comparing current performance to leading individuals or organizations (e.g., "How are we doing relative to our best competitors?")

Goal standards: comparing current performance to publicly stated goals (e.g., "How are we doing compared to the aspirational goals we have established?")

Improvement standards: comparing current performance with improvements made in the past (e.g., "How are we doing compared to our past improvement trends?")

Ideal standards: comparing current performance with an ideal or perfect standard (e.g., "How are we doing relative to a zero-defect standard?")

Stakeholder expectations: comparing current performance with the expectations of customers, employees, or other stakeholders (e.g., "How are we doing in helping customers flourish?")

Activity
Creating Readiness Through Comparisons

To help create readiness for culture change and to identify aspirational standards, consider the following list of activities. Select two or three to implement as an initial step in fostering a culture change.

- Identify others doing the same tasks better than you are.
- Host visitors who can share feedback about your work environment.
- Sponsor learning events such as guest lectures, symposia, or conferences.
- Create study teams and task forces to identify best practices.

- Schedule visits to other sites or locations.
- Identify problems associated with the status quo and advantages of a change.
- Identify WIIFM—What's In It For Me—for those being affected.

Another way to create readiness for change is to change the language people in the organization use. Over and over again it has been shown that when new language is used, perspectives change. For example, Warren Bennis and Burt Nanus observed that the most successful leaders in education, government, business, the arts, and the military are those who have developed a special language in which the word *failure* does not appear.[6] Instead, they use alternative descriptors, such as *temporary slowdown, false start, miscue, error, blooper, stumble, foul-up, obstacle, disappointment,* or *nonsuccess.* These leaders use an alternative language in order to interpret reality for their organizations in a way that fosters a willingness to try again and promotes an inclination toward a culture of abundance.

For example, a variety of organizations refer to employees as *teammates, associates, family members,* or even (at the Ritz-Carlton hotel chain) *ladies and gentlemen.* This language is intended to establish a culture of behavioral expectations and values. At the Disney Corporation, employees were hired by "central casting," not the human resources department. They were referred to as "cast members"; regardless of their jobs, they wore "costumes," not uniforms; they served "guests" and "audience members," not tourists; they worked in "attractions," not offices, stores, or rides; they played "characters" in the show (even as groundskeepers), not merely worked in a job; during working hours, they were "onstage" and had to go "offstage" to relax, eat, or socialize.

The intent of an alternative language is to change the way individuals think about their work, their role, and their values. It places them in a mind-set that they would not have considered otherwise. Changing language helps unfreeze old interpretations and create new ones, and using positive language does that in a positive manner. You may have heard that making people uncomfortable creates readiness for change. Often that does work, but it also leads to defensiveness, fear, crisis, and negative reactions. Developing a culture of abundance, on the other hand, focuses on creating readiness in ways that unlock positive motivations rather than resistance and provides optimistic alternatives rather than fear.

Activity
Creating Readiness Through Language

Select alternative terms for important aspects of your organization or your workplace that capture the values, the feelings, and the culture that you want to reinforce. Most often these alternative terms are words, but you could also use logos or symbols. The intent is to use language or symbols

ate the culture that you want to build, as in
elow.

?ization	*Alternative Label*
Employees	Colleagues
Customers	Guests
Work space	Playground
Break space	Fun factory
Tasks	Games
Materials	Resources
Outcomes	Pursuit of perfection
Measures	Accountability
Media	Image builder

What language, logos, or symbols might you use to create readiness?

OVERCOMING RESISTANCE

Most changes are uncomfortable, but this is especially true of culture change. Deeply held beliefs and assumptions are challenged, not to mention the disruption of interpersonal relationships, power and status, and routine ways of behaving in organizations. Culture change is usually interpreted as a negative condition, so resistance is likely. The role of the positive leader is to overcome resistance and change it into positive energy.

One way to think of resistance is to use Kurt Lewin's field theory of change.[7] This theory uses force field analysis to diagnose and overcome resistance. According to

FIGURE 7

Force Field Analysis

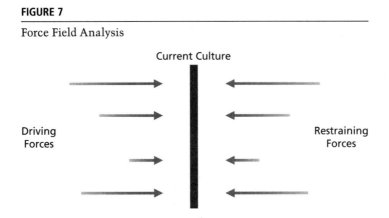

the theory, the current culture is a product of multiple forces working in opposite directions, as demonstrated in Figure 7.

On one side of the model are restraining forces, or resistance factors, that inhibit change. On the other side of the model are driving forces, or motivators, that encourage improvement and culture change. The culture is stable in its present form because the driving forces are exactly balanced with the restraining forces. The lines on each side of the Figure represent forces that are equal and balanced, explaining the organization's current culture.

Positive culture change results from an imbalance of forces. Overcoming resistance to culture change, therefore, involves weakening or eliminating restraining forces as well as strengthening and adding driving forces (see Figure 8).

FIGURE 8

Force Field Analysis and Culture Change

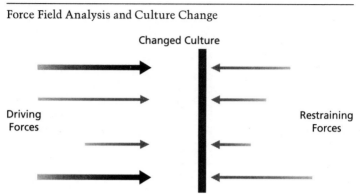

Changed Culture

Driving
Forces

Restraining
Forces

Reducing Restraining Forces

One well-known strategy for reducing resistance is to involve those who are most affected by the change. They can be asked to gather data, assist in implementation, help project outcomes and consequences, or communicate with others. Resistance is reduced when individuals believe that they have a say in the change agenda, have relevant information available to them, and are given some discretion or choice.

Another frequently used strategy is to find areas of common agreement between those who are pushing for change and those who are resisting it. This builds on the well-known negotiation technique of finding something on which the parties agree and then building from there. This is especially true when the advocates of change display empathy and understanding regarding the opposing point of view. Showing genuine caring for people who are resisting change helps preserve their self-esteem and avoids creating the impression that their point of view is irrelevant, ignorant, or invalid. Still another strategy is to highlight what will not change even after the new culture is developed. Reinforcing what is familiar and comfortable as well as what will be preserved help reduce ambiguity, uncertainty, and anxiety. Resistors can safeguard at least some elements of the culture that are familiar.

Increasing Driving Forces

A well-known strategy for enhancing and strengthening positive driving forces is to identify benefits, future opportunities, and desirable outcomes. For example, what advantages will be provided by the new culture? A related technique is to highlight past successes and achievements that are linked with the preferred culture. For example, what evidence exists that a change toward the new culture leads to more success or more opportunities to flourish?

The more power and prestige held by the champions of change, the less resistance there will be among other members of the organization. Therefore, another strategy for strengthening driving forces is to obtain the support of powerful or influential individuals, build coalitions of recognized or admired people, and create "change teams" consisting of positively energizing people. People who uplift and energize others can help reduce resistance by being messengers and advocates.

Bennis, Benne, and Chin found that individuals would rather follow leaders who display a consistent set of values—even if they disagree with those values—than leaders whose values are ambiguous or unstable[8] Lawrence Kohlberg found that the most influential change agents are those who display a consistent, comprehensive, universalistic set of values that clarify what they stand for.[9] Thus, another strategy for increasing driving forces is to clarify and exemplify a core set of values and virtues upon which the new abundance culture will be based. Because virtuousness is heliotropic, people are inclined to follow leaders who create a culture based on core values and virtues.

Activity
Overcoming Resistance

The lists below illustrate some ways to overcome resistance. For your own organization, identify practices that will reduce resistance forces as well as increase drive forces.

Reduce Restraining Forces
- Involve others
- Find areas of agreement
- Identify what won't change

Increase Driving Forces
- Identify benefits
- Form coalitions and identify champions
- Establish and demonstrate a core set of values

ARTICULATING A VISION OF ABUNDANCE

When you have created readiness and reduced resistance, the people in your organization still need to know what the new culture will be like. This is where articulating a vision of abundance comes in: picturing the organization as a source of flourishing and as an entity that creates a legacy about which people care deeply. This kind of vision helps unleash human potential, since it addresses the basic human desire to do something that makes a difference, something that has enduring impact.

Visions of abundance are different from visions of goal achievement or effectiveness, such as earning a certain level of profit, becoming number one in the marketplace, or receiving recognition. Rather, a vision of abundance speaks to the heart as well as the head. It attracts people by appealing to both the left and right sides of the human brain and by making the vision interesting.

Appealing to Both Sides of the Brain

The brain is divided into two halves. The left hemisphere controls rational, cognitive activities such as sequential thinking, logic, deduction, numeric thought, and so on. Activities such as reading, solving math problems, and rational analysis are dominated by left-brain thinking. The right hemisphere, in contrast, controls nonrational cognitive activities such as intuition, creativity, fantasy, emotions, pictorial images, and imagination. Composing music, storytelling, and artistic creation are tied to right-brain thinking.

Neither hemisphere operates autonomously from the other, and this illustrates why vision statements must appeal to both left-brain and right-brain elements. Targets, goals, and action plans (left-brain components) must be supplemented by metaphors, colorful language, and imagination (right-brain components). Unfortunately, most organizational vision statements are almost exclusively left-brain dominant. They focus much more on objectives, processes, and desired outcomes than they do on emotions, imagery, and virtue.

To articulate the left-brain elements of the vision for your organization, answer the following questions:

- What are our most important strengths as an organization?
- Where do we have a strategic advantage?
- What major problems and obstacles do we need to address?
- What stands in the way of significant improvement?
- What are the primary resources that we need?
- What information do we require?
- Who are our key customers?
- What must be done to respond to stakeholder expectations?
- What measurable outcomes will we accomplish?
- What are the criteria to be monitored?

To articulate the right-brain elements of the vision for your organization, answer the following questions:

- What is the highest aspiration we can achieve?
- What have we done in the past that represents spectacularly positive performance?
- What stories can we tell or events can we describe that illustrate what we stand for?
- What metaphors or analogies can we use that epitomize our ideal future?
- What symbols are appropriate for helping capture people's imaginations?
- What colorful and inspirational language can exemplify what we believe in?
- What logos or images can people rally around?
- What do we care most deeply about that should be pursued?

Making It Interesting

Murray Davis published a now classic article on what causes some kinds of information to be judged interesting while other information is uninteresting.[10] The veracity of the information has little to do with that judgment, according to Davis. Rather, the degree to which information is interesting depends on the extent to which it contradicts weakly held assumptions and challenges the status quo. If new information is consistent with what is already known, people tend to dismiss it as common sense—it is not interesting. If new information is obviously contradictory to strongly held assumptions, or if it blatantly challenges the core values of the organization's members, it is labeled ridiculous, silly, or blasphemous—and it is also dismissed as not interesting. What is considered interesting is information that helps create new ways to view the future, challenges the current state of things but not core values, and lifts people's thinking into new realms of what is possible. Interesting information draws people in and creates new insights or uncovers a new way to think.

Visions of abundance are interesting. They contain challenges and prods that confront and alter the ways people think about the past and the future. They are not extreme or threatening in their message, just provocative. Visions such as "a man on the moon by the end of the decade" (President John F. Kennedy), "corporate immortality" (Ralph Peterson, CEO of CH2M HILL), "perfect service" (Mike McCallister, CEO of Humana), and "one person, one computer" (Steve Jobs, founder and CEO of Apple) were all visions that challenged the status quo, but not in outlandish ways. They identified a message that people cared about but which challenged the normal perception of things. The fact that their messages are interesting is what captured attention and positive energy.

Activity
Vision of Abundance

Think of inspiring vision statements you have encountered. Examples might include Martin Luther King Jr.'s "I Have a Dream" speech (http://historywired.si.edu/detail.cfm?ID=501), Nelson Mandela's "An Ideal for Which I Am Prepared to Die" speech (http://db.nelsonmandela.org/speeches/pub_view.asp?pg=item&itemID=NMS010&txtstr=1963), or Winston Churchill's

"Never Give In" speech (http://www.winstonchurchill.org /learn/speeches/speeches-of-winston-churchill/103-never-give-in). Write a simple paragraph articulating your own vision of abundance. This can be for your organization or for yourself. Make certain that you include at least one story, metaphor, or image. This is not a statement of goal setting or problem solving; rather, it is a statement that leads to abundance. Address this question: "Based on what we/I care most deeply about, what is the highest and most inspiring aspiration we/I can achieve?"

Consider the example of a vision articulated by John Scully, who took over for Steve Jobs in the very early days of Apple Computer's existence in 1987. It provides just one example of abundance:

> We are all part of a journey to create an extraordinary corporation. The things we intend to do in the years ahead have never been done before. . . . One person, one computer is still our dream. . . . We want to make personal computers a way of life in work, education, and the home. Apple people are paradigm shifters. . . . We want to be the catalyst for discovering new ways for people to do things. . . . Apple's way starts with a passion to create awesome products with a lot of distinctive value built in. . . . We have chosen directions for Apple that will lead us to wonderful ideas we haven't as yet dreamed.[11]

GENERATING COMMITMENT

Once the vision of abundance has been articulated, positive leaders must help organization members become committed to the vision—to adopt the vision as their own and to work toward its accomplishment. The whole intent of a vision statement is to mobilize the energy and potential of the individuals who are to implement it and who will be affected by it. Developing a culture of abundance depends on commitment to a vision of abundance.

Identify Small Wins

We are all more committed to winners than to losers. Fans attend more games when the team has a good record than when it has a poor record. The number of people claiming to have voted for a winning candidate always exceeds by a large margin the actual number of votes received. In other words, when we see success or progress being made, we are more committed to respond positively, to continue that path, and to offer our support.[12]

Leaders of positive culture change create this kind of commitment by identifying and publicizing small wins. These can be things as minor as a new coat of paint, abolishing reserved parking spaces, adding a display case for awards, flying a flag, holding social events, instituting a suggestion system, and so on. A small wins strategy is designed to create a sense of progress and momentum by creating minor, quick changes. The basic rule of thumb for small wins is this: Find something that is easy to change. Change it. Publicize it, or recognize it publicly. Then find a second thing that is easy to change, and repeat the process.

Small wins create commitment because (1) they reduce the importance of any one change ("It's no big deal to make this change"), (2) they reduce demands on any group or individual ("There's not a lot we have to do"), (3) they improve the confidence of participants ("I can do that"), (4) they help avoid resistance or retaliation ("Even if I disagree, it's only a small thing"), (5) they attract allies and create a bandwagon effect ("I want to be associated with this success"), (6) they create the image of progress ("Things seem to be moving forward"), (7) if they do not work there are no long-lasting effects ("If it doesn't pan out, there's no major harm done"), and (8) they provide initiatives in multiple arenas, reducing the chance of resistance forming in one ("I can't say no to all of them").

Demonstrating Public Commitment

Making a public declaration motivates individuals to do what they have said they will do.[13] After making public pronouncements, individuals are much more committed to and more consistent in the behavior they have espoused.[14]

For example, during World War II, good cuts of meat were in short supply in the United States. Kurt Lewin found that a significant difference existed between the commitment level of shoppers who promised out loud to buy more plentiful but less desirable cuts of meat (e.g., liver, kidneys, brains) compared to those who made the same promise in private. In another study, students in a college class were divided into two groups. All students set goals for how much they would read and what kinds of scores they would get on exams. Only half the students were allowed to state these goals publicly to the rest of the class. By midsemester, the students who stated their goals publicly averaged an 86 percent improvement. The students who only set their goals privately averaged a 14 percent improvement.[15]

Leaders creating a culture of abundance look for opportunities to have others make public statements in favor of the vision or to restate the vision themselves. Assigning individuals to explain the vision to the public, to outside groups, to other employees, or to family members provides opportunities for them to put the vision in their own words. Discussion groups that encourage members to refine or clarify the vision also provide opportunities for public commitment.

Activity
Generating Commitment

As you consider your desired culture of abundance, identify two or three small things that can be easily and readily changed and that will make progress toward that culture—what could be altered beginning Monday morning? What has been accomplished so far—what minor victories can you highlight, and how can you publicize them? What opportunities can you provide for people to publicly express their commitment? Take a few minutes to identify one or two ideas for creating small wins and for generating commitment.

FOSTERING SUSTAINABILITY

The fifth step in the culture change process is intended to push culture change deeper into the organization, ensuring that that culture of abundance becomes institutionalized and can be sustained over time. Culture change will be sustainable when the change extends beyond merely surface-level behavior, and values, ideology, and preferences change at a fundamental level. The United States Army refers to this step as "creating irreversible momentum," ensuring that positive change is institutionalized so strongly that it cannot be thwarted. The challenge is to separate the vision from the visionary—to get all members of the organization to own and become champions of the change, and to create processes that reinforce the positive change without having to continually rely on the leader. Even if the leader leaves, the positive change will continue because sustainable momentum is in place.

Fostering sustainability does not happen quickly, of course, and the four previous steps in developing a culture of abundance—creating readiness, overcoming resistance, articulating a vision, and generating commitment—must be successfully accomplished first. Sustainability is the final step to ensure that a cultural change will actually occur over time, since culture does not change quickly.

Metrics, Measures, and Milestones

Metrics (specific indicators of success), measures (methods for assessing levels of success), and milestones (benchmarks to determine when detectable progress has occurred) are key to ensuring that change is sustainable. These three factors help guarantee accountability for change, make it clear how much progress is being made, and provide visible indicators that the change is successful. The adage "You get what you measure" is an illustration of this principle. Change becomes sustainable when it is part of what people are held accountable to achieve. Sustaining positive change, then, means that clear metrics are identified, a measurement system is put into place, and a milestone is specified for when the change has been accomplished.

Stories

Culture change is more likely to be sustainable if it is carried and communicated through stories. Just as right-brain elements must be a part of vision statements, culture change must rely on stories to be sustainable.[16] The key values, desired orientations, and behavioral principles that are to characterize the new culture are usually more clearly communicated through stories than in any other way. The values and virtues that employees are to exemplify in the new culture are best explained and demonstrated by telling and retelling stories that illustrate the desired behaviors. Ideal stories draw on real experiences, show personal involvement, and illustrate the key attributes of the culture of abundance. The stories do not need to be numerous; just one or two may be sufficient to communicate the desired culture of abundance.

Social Support

People are in most need of social support when they are in the middle of change and uncertainty.[17] Culture change is a time when supportive interpersonal relationships are especially critical. Therefore, social events, gatherings, and collective activities are important for fostering sustainability. Building coalitions of supporters and empowering them to communicate and demonstrate key cultural values are also helpful. Especially, identifying and engaging positive energizers and those who will be most affected by the changes deserves special attention. Champions who can influence the opinions of others and serve as role models for the virtues and values associated with an abundance culture must be visible and active.

Leadership

Positive leaders must have the skills to create the consensus and collaboration required for any organization to sustain change. Positive leaders must also develop the competencies necessary to sustain the organization once it has actually developed the desired culture of abundance. They must both lead the change process and be able to reinforce and support the changes that have occurred.

Leaders also must demonstrate personal commitment to and responsibility for the change. One way to do this is to make a visible "sacrifice"—that is, publicly give up something of value (financial, symbolic, or structural) that is associated with the current culture in favor of something that embodies the values and virtues of the new culture. A visible personal sacrifice by the leader not only demonstrates personal responsibility for the change but communicates authenticity, sincerity, and a genuine devotion to the new culture.

Activity
Fostering Sustainability

Consider the following questions that can help ensure sustainable culture change in your organization:

Metrics: What are the key indicators of culture change? How do we know culture change is occurring? What are the indicators of progress toward culture change?

Measures: How will we gather information about our new culture? What will we assess?

Milestones: When will we expect to see noticeable culture change?

Stories: What incidents or events illustrate the key virtues, values, and attributes that will characterize our new culture of abundance? When have we demonstrated this kind of culture in the past?

Social support: In what ways can we bring people together? How can involvement and consensus be facilitated? What can we do to foster stronger social relationships? Who needs to come together to champion the culture change?

Leadership: Where are we strong, and where are we in need of leadership development? What leadership development activities should we sponsor to help leaders build the needed competencies and behaviors? What meaningful and visible sacrifice could be made?

CONCLUSION

Organizations that flourish have developed a culture of abundance, one that both allows its members to flourish personally and makes it possible for the organization to achieve extraordinarily positive performance. The steps described here are not comprehensive, of course, nor do they represent the only possible path toward a culture of abundance. Other models of change and many more suggestions for culture change are available.[18] On the other hand, both empirical evidence and multiple intervention experiences in organizations have confirmed that the tools outlined here are an effective way to help develop a culture of abundance in organizations.

3
HOW TO DEVELOP POSITIVE ENERGY NETWORKS

At the heart of positive leadership lies the concept of positive energy. Whereas much popular literature is dominated by discussions about the toll of stress, burnout, depression, tension, anxiety, fatigue, disengagement, and fear, less attention is paid to positive energy, even though it is one of the most powerful and important predictors of organizational and individual success. It is almost impossible to be a positive leader without also being a source of positive energy.

This chapter summarizes evidence that positively energizing leaders create extraordinarily high performance in their organizations and in their people. It provides some tools and practices that have been successfully applied in a variety of settings, such as those associated with recreational work, contributions, and mapping energy networks.

Positive energy is characterized by a feeling of aliveness, arousal, vitality, and zest. It is the life-giving force that allows us to perform, to create, and to persist. It unlocks resources and capacity within us and actually increases our ability to flourish.[1] Positive energy is probably the single most important attribute of positive leaders.

TYPES OF ENERGY

To learn how to foster positive energy, we have to distinguish among several familiar but different types of energy: physical, psychological, and emotional. In the human body, *physical energy* is associated with the interaction between glucose, the substance that provides the energy for our cells, and adenosine triphosphate (ATP), a molecule our cells produce that captures that energy and delivers it to where it is needed.[2] Activity, whether it is running a marathon or merely working a long, difficult day, depletes the body of these substances, and we have to restore them through nourishment, relaxation, and sleep.

Psychological energy is associated with mental concentration and cognitive focus. When intense mental effort is expended—as when studying for an exam or engaging in extended concentration on a challenging problem—we become mentally fatigued. Most of us have experienced being so tired that it is difficult even to think. Psychological energy is replenished by mental breaks, relaxation, and by changing the focus of attention to something less tedious.

Emotional energy is associated with the experience of intense feelings. As with physical and psychological energy, emotional energy can be depleted—for example, by impassioned excitement in an athletic contest, intense sadness at the loss of a family member, or the breakup of a relationship—and must then be replenished. Burnout is an example of emotional exhaustion, and like other forms of energy, we need recuperation to replenish and restore this form of energy.

In contrast to these three types of energy, which become depleted when used, *relational energy* actually increases as it is exercised. Expressing and receiving relational energy through positive interpersonal relationships uplifts, invigorates, and rejuvenates us. It increases rather than diminishes as it is expended. Consider the times you have interacted with a person with whom you have a loving, supportive relationship. Your energy is not diminished or exhausted as a result of the interaction; rather it is renewed and augmented. Experiencing love, nurturing, and support is life-giving rather than life-depleting.

The question this chapter addresses is how leaders of organizations can utilize this positive relational energy and enable others to use it as well.

ENERGY AND MOTIVATION

At first glance, you might think that positive energy is the same thing as mere motivation. A common assumption is that the key challenge of a leader is to motivate others, and indeed there is a large literature on motivation and incentives. However, motivation and energy are not synonymous. Theories of motivation seldom acknowledge energy as the driving force behind action and performance. Instead, they usually assume that people are motivated by need fulfillment, by goals, or by cognitive evaluations.

For example, one set of motivation theories suggests that people are motivated by unfulfilled needs. These needs include *existence* needs, such as personal safety and physiological needs; *relatedness* or social needs, such as belonging, affiliation, or self-esteem needs; and *growth* needs, such as self-actualization and meaning needs.[3] Other authors have postulated that the need for *power* and the need for *achievement* are the bases of motivation.[4] In these theories, an unfulfilled need serves as a motivator. (The exception is self-actualization or growth needs, in which fulfilled needs lead to more motivation.)

Another set of theories suggests that the presence of goals serves to motivate performance. People are motivated by having a clear target or objective that guides task accomplishment. These theories draw on the assumption that if we want high performance, we almost always establish goals as a way to attain it. Goals give people something to strive for.[5]

A third set of motivation theories, called expectancy theories, suggest that people make cognitive evaluations regarding the circumstances they encounter and are motivated to act based on their appraisal of those circumstances. Specifically, if we have the *ability* (meaning the aptitude, training, and resources) to succeed, if we have the *expectation* that by expending effort we can succeed, and if we feel that the task is *worthwhile* or that it is important, we will be motivated. Cognitive evaluation of each of these various factors is required—though it can be subconscious—for motivation to be present.[6]

Another example of a cognitive theory associated with motivation is the social comparison theory. Simply put, if I think that I am being treated fairly—for example, if my compensation is similar to that of colleagues doing the same job—I will be motivated. If someone else is being paid more than I for the same work, I will be demotivated.[7]

None of these motivation theories acknowledges energy as a key source of activation or of enhanced task performance. It is true that leaders and managers must ensure that employees' needs are met—for example, ensuring a safe and pleasant working environment, ensuring satisfying team dynamics, and providing opportunities for challenge and growth. They must establish goals, targets, and benchmarks against which performance can be measured. They must ensure fair and equitable compensation. And they must make it possible for employees to see the outcomes of their work and experience them as worthwhile. That is, they must manage need fulfillment, goal setting, and people's expectancies.

However, positive energy is an even more important factor in accounting for high performance. While much of the leadership literature equates leadership and influence (people who influence others are shown to be higher performers)[8] and maintains that information is a key attribute of leaders (people who are more informed and knowledgeable than others tend to have higher performance), research has confirmed that positive energy is four times more important in predicting performance than either influence or information. Positive energy trumps most other factors in accounting for organizational success.

Beryl Health, a call center in Texas, is three to four times more profitable than the industry average and enjoys miniscule employee turnover rates. CEO Paul Spiegelman attributes the firm's success to the development and reinforcement of positive energy in the company. He has appointed one of his senior corporate officers as "Queen of Fun and Growth," and her role is to organize family fun days and holiday carnivals as well as to foster a climate of non-stop positively energizing interactions. The payoff for Beryl is customer loyalty, fast growth, and a "Best Places to Work" designation.[9]

THE IMPORTANCE OF ENERGY

My colleagues and I conducted studies in four large organizations with the purpose of assessing positive energy in unit leaders.[10] Measuring positive energy is best achieved by asking individuals to assess the extent to which they are personally energized as a result of interacting with another person. As an example, I would rate the extent to which I feel energized and uplifted when I interact with you. Note that I am not rating the extent to which I think you are a positive energizer; rather, I am rating my own feelings and responses. This is a subtle but important distinction. Measuring energy is a personal assessment. I do not know if you are experiencing positive energy, only that I am. So when we measure energy, we ask people to rate their own energy level when interacting with other individuals.

In our study, we found that five items form a reliable and valid measure of positive energy, and you may want to use this scale to assess positive leadership energy in your own organization:

1. I feel invigorated when I interact with this person.
2. After interacting with this person I feel more energy to do my work.
3. I feel increased vitality when I interact with this person.
4. I would go to this person when I need to be "pepped up."
5. After an exchange with this person I feel more stamina to do my work.

The findings from this study revealed that when individuals are exposed to a positively energizing leader in their workplace, they have significantly higher personal well-being, higher satisfaction with their jobs, higher engagement in their organization, higher job performance, and higher levels of family well-being than those without exposure to positively energizing leaders. Moreover, the organizational unit in which these people work has significantly more cohesion among employees, more orientation toward learning, more expression of experimentation and creativity, and higher levels of performance than units without an energizing leader.[11] The impact of having an energizing leader at work, in other words, was found to be extremely strong.

These findings are consistent with the research of Cole, Bruch, and Vogel, who found that positive energy is strongly related to individual goal achievement, engagement, job satisfaction, and firm performance across five different countries.[12] They are also reinforced by studies confirming that individuals who positively energize others are higher performers themselves.[13]

Moreover, positively energized people are more adaptive, more creative, suffer from fewer physical illnesses and accidents, and experience richer interpersonal relationships than others. People tend to avoid and limit their communication with de-energizers, whereas they are attracted to positive energizers.[14]

CHARACTERISTICS OF POSITIVE ENERGIZERS

It is important to note that being a positive energizer is *not* the same as being an extrovert, gregarious, charismatic, or perky. The correlation between the Big 5 personality attributes (which include the extraversion-introversion dimension) and positive energy, for example, is low and non-significant. Being the first to speak, the one who dominates airtime, or the social butterfly is not necessarily positively energizing for others. Rather, positive energy is associated with a set of behaviors that are mostly interactive and behavioral and which can be learned and developed.

Listed below are attributes identified by executives when describing positive energizers in their organizations. It is not a comprehensive list, of course, but note that each of these attributes can be cultivated.

Energizers	*De-energizers*
They help other people flourish.	They mostly see roadblocks and obstacles.
They are trustworthy and have integrity.	They create problems.
They are dependable.	They do not allow others to be valued.
They use abundance language.	They are inflexible in their thinking.
They are heedful and fully engaged.	They do not show concern for others.
They are genuine and authentic.	They often do not follow through.
They see opportunities.	They are self-aggrandizing.
They solve problems.	They are mostly somber and solemn.
They smile.	They are superficial and inauthentic.
They express gratitude and humility.	They are frequently critical.

The activities listed in the rest of the chapter do not address these attributes individually; rather, they are designed to address positive energy in general and help you foster more positive energy in yourself, as well as to utilize positive energy networks in your organization.

DEVELOPING POSITIVE ENERGY

Because positive energy is synonymous with relational energy, building and nurturing strong interpersonal relationships is a key to fostering and maintaining positive energy.

Value-Added Contributions

Strong interpersonal relationships are most easily built on a foundation of positive feedback rather than criticism. Rather than pointing out weaknesses and deficiencies, positive leaders highlight others' strengths, capabilities, and contributions and enable others in the organization to do the same. This does not mean being inauthentic or oblivious to flaws, rather it means highlighting the unique expertise upon which others can build.

Activity
Value-Added Contributions

This activity provides an opportunity to identify personal strengths and the contributions of unit members as well as to help individuals unleash latent positive energy in your organization.

1. Feedback

Provide each member of your organization or unit with one blank card or piece of paper for each other member of the organization or unit. For example, if there are ten members of the unit, each member receives nine cards—one for each person in the unit minus him- or herself. For each member's batch of cards, write the name of each of the other members of the unit on one of the cards. (You can put the name of the person giving the feedback at the bottom of each card, but this is optional.)

On one side of the card, address this issue for the person whose name is on the card: *Here are the special contributions that you make to our unit. Here are the unique strengths and capabilities that you demonstrate. Here is what I value regarding you and your contribution.*

On the reverse side of the card, address this issue for the same person: *If we are to become extraordinary, exceed our aspirations, become the benchmark organization, and achieve positive deviance in our performance, here is what else we need from you. Here is the positive energy you can provide. Here are the contributions you can make.*

2. Distribution

Once all the comments have been written down, distribute each card to the individual whose name is on the card. In a ten-person unit, each person should have nine cards. Read the cards with your name at the top, identify the themes and the key points in the feedback those cards contain, and write down your interpretation and response.

3. Interpretations

Write at least one paragraph summarizing your interpretations of the feedback from the first side of the card. Address these questions: *What do others especially value about my leadership capabilities? In what ways have I made important and unique contributions? In what ways do I add value? What do others most admire about me? What are my unique strengths?*

Write at least one more paragraph summarizing your interpretations of the feedback from the second side of the card. This paragraph should contain your view of the expectations others have for you in order to enhance performance. *In what ways can I add positive energy to the unit? If we are to attain our highest potential, and if we are to achieve dramatic success, here is what I need to do. Here is how I can contribute more. Here is how I can capitalize on my strengths.*

4. Public Commitments

Read the paragraphs you have written to the other members of the unit. Highlight your commitments for adding value, fostering positive energy, and enabling success. Especially make sure that you identify how you will maintain accountability for following through. Ask other members of the unit to help ensure that you fulfill the commitments you have made in public.

CONTEMPLATIVE PRACTICE

A second way to enhance personal positive energy is through contemplative practices. Now, before you dismiss this as a New Age detour from an otherwise scientifically based approach to positive leadership, consider some recent research that has examined the impact of contemplative practice, especially loving-kindness meditation, on positive energy, positive emotions, and positive relationships.[15] Neuroscientists have recently discovered, for example, that the brain actually changes as the result of our thoughts and experiences (a phenomenon referred to as *neuroplasticity*). In one study, Fredrickson and colleagues conducted a controlled experiment in which some people engaged in six weeks of loving-kindness meditation—designed to help people develop more warmth and tenderness toward themselves and others— and a control group that did not.

Loving-kindness meditation is a well-developed contemplative practice that focuses on self-generated feelings of love, compassion, and goodwill toward oneself and others. Essentially, people contemplate their feelings of positive regard for people close to them and extend them outward to others not so close to them. Similar practices include keeping a "gratitude journal," engaging in personal prayer, and pondering spiritual inspiration. These practices essentially put people in a virtuous condition in which they represent the best of the human condition on a recurring basis.

The results of Fredrickson's research are compelling. Dramatic differences were noted in brain functioning, vagal tone (the strength of the heart-body connection that controls cardiovascular and immune responses), and social energy.[16] Furthermore, other studies show that regular meditation diminishes stress-related cortisol, insomnia, symptoms of autoimmune illnesses, PMS, asthma, falling back into depression, general emotional distress, anxiety, and panic. Meditation tends to help control blood sugar in type 2 diabetics, increases detachment from negative reactions, enhances self-understanding, and increases general well-being. Links have also been uncovered with various infections and chronic conditions such as high blood pressure, obesity, cancer, and heart disease.[17]

Regular contemplative practices are linked to increases in gray matter in the areas of the brain that control learning, memory, emotional regulation, self-referential processing, and perspective taking. In other words, contemplative practice literally changes the physical structure of the brain. Self-awareness, empathy for the emotions of others, and the reduction of cortical thinning due to aging all are enhanced.[18]

In an important finding, researchers discovered a strong interactive relationship between loving-kindness meditation, positive social connections, vagal tone, and positive energy. Positive energy was enhanced when people engaged in loving-kindness meditation, even for short periods of time.[19] Practicing loving-kindness meditation for just seven minutes per day for several weeks was found to markedly increase social connectedness and relational energy.[20]

Activity
Contemplative Practice

Designate some time each day (as little as three minutes to as much as thirty minutes) to engage in a contemplative practice.

Loving-kindness meditation, in brief, requires that you put yourself in a relaxed and quiet state, then focus on your feelings of love, warmth, and positive regard for those closest to you, such as family members. Eventually you extend these feelings outward to those who are less close to you, such as friends and acquaintances.

Alternatively, you can maintain a gratitude journal, recording on a daily basis the things for which you are most grateful and/or the good things that happened to you. You can also spend time contemplating the people to whom you are the closest and recalling the things you love and admire about them, the gifts they have given you, and the ways they give you joy. A third option is to engage in personal prayer, in which you acknowledge and thank God for blessings, strengths, talents, and opportunities. These and similar activities have been shown in controlled experiments to produce remarkably positive consequences, especially if you are consistent in practicing them.

FUN AND RECREATION

In a variety of experiments in Europe, researchers demonstrated how making normally routine activities fun markedly altered the behavior and energy of people. Several of these experiments are visually described at www.thefuntheory.com. For example, 66 percent more people took the stairs than the adjoining escalator after experimenters made the stairs look like a piano keyboard with sounds associated with each step. More than a hundred people recycled glass bottles in a container that provided video-game sounds when a bottle was deposited, compared to only two people using a normal container nearby. Over two and a half times more trash was deposited in a waste can that provided a sound simulating the deposit falling hundreds of feet followed by a boom than in a nearby ordinary waste can. The experimenters demonstrated that making routine activities fun provides a positive experience, engenders positive energy, and alters behavior for the better.

Positive energy and fun are connected.[21] Engaging in fun or novel activities not only breaks up routine and boredom but also fosters and enables positive energy, especially when the fun is connected with interpersonal relationships.

You may have heard the truism "People are willing to pay for the privilege of working harder than they will work when they are paid."[22] Consider what happens around mid-November in Utah and Colorado when the first major snowfall graces the ski resorts. Work and school absenteeism skyrockets. People sacrifice a day's pay, don their $400 skis, their $300 boots, and their $250 ski outfit, buy $80 in gasoline to drive to the nearest ski resort, pay $115 for a lift ticket, eat a $35 hot dog for lunch, and return at the end of the day completely exhausted—having paid for the privilege of working harder than they would work when they are paid.

The question is, why? Why do people spend money to exhaust themselves, endure uncomfortable environmental conditions, and put their bodies at risk when they would not accept the same amount of money to do those things at work? The answer is obvious: because it is fun, not work.

The attributes that make activities fun, however, can be as typical of work as they are of leisure:[23]

Goals are positive and clearly defined: Recreation is always associated with a goal—winning a game, shooting a low (or high) score, challenging a personal best, improving performance. It is fun to work toward a positive goal. By contrast, the goal of simply avoid losing is not positively energizing, and activity just for the sake of activity rarely lasts. Positive goals make activities fun.

Scorekeeping is objective and self-administered: In recreation, we always know the score. When we do not keep score, we soon lose interest. Even on playgrounds, unorganized activity almost always eventually finds itself organizing into a game where scorekeeping occurs. In athletic contests, when the scoreboard stops working or players lose track of who is ahead, the game usually stops.

Feedback is frequent: In almost all recreation, we know how we are doing at any given moment. That is why organized athletics is played in the presence of fans. Their feedback makes it fun. Home field advantage matters.

Personal choice exists: In recreation, we have the chance to modify our behavior at will. We are not constrained to a specific routine or process that cannot be modified. Being empowered to alter performance is positively energizing when we are doing fun things.

Rules are standard and stable: In recreation the rules are always clear. Out of bounds is always out of bounds. A goal is always a goal. Effort and difficulty do not determine the outcomes. In baseball, a spectacular catch still counts for only one out.

Competition is present: Competition can be against personal past performance or against others, but we always have more fun when we are tested against a standard. If you are an adult, playing ball against third graders is not fun for very long because it is not challenging or competitive.

Social interaction is fostered: Bowling leagues arise because bowling alone is no fun. People play golf in foursomes because playing alone does not provide much positive energy. Recreation and fun are almost always associated with the chance to socialize and interact.

Activity
Recreational Work

Here are a dozen suggestions for experiencing fun and enabling positive energy. Select one or two activities that appeal to you (or come up with your own) and commit to personally engage, or help your organization engage, in them this week.

- Play a game, any game.
- Redesign your work so that it contains attributes of recreation.
- Visit one place you have not visited before.

- Spend time with children.
- Spend some time in the natural, non-built environment.
- Sing.
- Sponsor a social event (even lunch) to which several people are invited.
- Laugh with someone.
- Engage at least once in whole-body physical exercise.
- Learn one new thing.
- Write a gratitude message to one new person.
- Surprise someone with a gift.

ASSESSING POSITIVE ENERGY NETWORKS

One of the key questions about positive energy is how it can be measured. How do you know who are the positive energizers in your organization, and how can you influence the amount of positive energy available? Diagramming a positive energy network is one way to address this issue.

Most of us are familiar with network maps—for example, we see route maps in the back of airline magazines or in bus or subway stations. They show connections among cities or stations, with some being at the center or hub of the network and some being on the periphery. The same kind of network map can be constructed to identify positive energizers, only instead of cities or stations, people are the nodes, and the lines drawn between them represent their relationships. Energy networks help identify which people serve as hubs in the network and which people are on the periphery. The research is clear that positive energizers—or hubs in the network—are not only higher performers themselves but also help elevate others' performance.[24]

Three options exist for assessing positive energy networks: statistical mapping, a bubble chart, and a pulse survey.

Statistical Mapping

The most rigorous and sophisticated way to create a positive energy network map is to use statistical software. UCINET, a software application designed to construct network maps, can be downloaded from the Web (www.analytictech.com), and it is not difficult to understand and apply.

To use the software, provide a list of organization (or unit) members to each person in the organization (or unit). Ask each person to use a seven-point scale to evaluate his or her interaction with each of the other persons on the list.

> When I interact with _____, what happens to my energy?
>
> 1 = I am very de-energized
> 2 = I am moderately de-energized
> 3 = I am slightly de-energized
> 4 = I am neither energized nor de-energized
> 5 = I am slightly positively energized
> 6 = I am moderately positively energized
> 7 = I am very positively energized

The numbers associated with each name are recorded in the UCINET software, producing an analysis

FIGURE 9

A Network Map

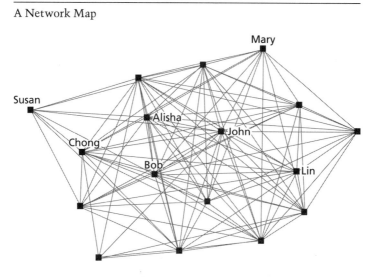

such as the one shown in Figure 9. This particular network map includes only the names of people who received ratings of 6 or 7—in other words, people who were rated as positively energizing.

The connecting lines show how many organization members are positively energized when interacting with each person. The more connecting lines, the more central the person is in the positive energy network. The highest energizers appear in the center of the network diagram. (It is possible, of course, to also create a map identifying those who received scores of 1 or 2. These are the folks who are de-energizers and tend to suck the life out of other members of the organization.)

UCINET also produces a "density score" showing the percentage of possible energizing ties that are present. Of all possible energizing connections, how many actually exist? The greater the percentage of all possible energizing ties that exist, the more effective the organization. (By contrast, the greater the density of de-energizing ties, the less effective the organization.)

One use of energy networks was illustrated by Prudential Financial Corporation, in which employee "change teams" were created to help disseminate information and conduct training associated with a major culture change initiative. The change team members were selected on the basis of their position in the positive energy network, with the highest positive energizers picked for the team. As might be expected, by using a team of positive energizers, the culture change initiative was implemented much more effectively and much more rapidly than normal.

Activity
Network Mapping

Download the UCINET software from www.analytictech.com; instructions are available online. Distribute to each member of your organization (or unit) a list of all members' names. (This can include a large or small number of people inasmuch as network maps have been created with hundreds of people. You will want to identify the organizational unit that is of most interest to you.)

Have each member of the organization respond to the following question regarding every other person:

When I interact with _____, what happens to my energy?

1 = I am very de-energized
2 = I am moderately de-energized
3 = I am slightly de-energized
4 = I am neither energized nor de-energized
5 = I am slightly positively energized
6 = I am moderately positively energized
7 = I am very positively energized

Input the data into the software to create an energy network map of the organization. Analyze the network by addressing the following questions:

- Who are the most positively energizing people in the organization?
- What is the density of the energy network, and how can it be enhanced?
- What are the key personal attributes of our most positively energizing people?
- What rewards or recognition should be given to those demonstrating high positive energy?
- What mentoring relationships should be created to take advantage of the positive energizers?
- What teams should be formed to capitalize on the positive energy network?
- What kinds of activities can be conducted to foster more positive energy in the organization?
- What are the leadership training and development implications for the organization?
- What implications for succession planning are implied by this energy network?

In providing feedback using this kind of map, be careful that you do not attach names to the nodes on the map—seeing that one's position in the energy network is not as expected can cause emotional turmoil or embarrassment. Just use the map to give people a sense of how the organization is functioning, and then use the data to follow up with individuals who are in need of energy development and with individuals whose energy can be better utilized in the group or organization. Positively energizing teams can also be formed using those in the center of the network.

Bubble Chart

A second way to assess positive energy without using a statistical software package is to merely ask organization members to write down the names of the three people (or whatever number you think is appropriate) whom they would rate as the most positive, energizing people in the organization. Then tally the votes and create bubbles whose relative sizes represent the number of votes each person received. This will help you identify the positive energizers in your organization quickly.

The disadvantage of this technique, of course, is that you do not see the totality of the network ties, the density of the network, or the people who are de-energizers or "black holes." It is just a simple and quick way to identify positive energizers in your organization. If Figure 10 represented the map of your own unit, for example, you would want to think carefully about recognizing and

FIGURE 10

A Positive Energy Bubble Chart

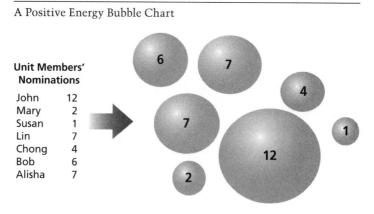

**Unit Members'
Nominations**

John	12
Mary	2
Susan	1
Lin	7
Chong	4
Bob	6
Alisha	7

rewarding the energizing people, forming mentoring re-lationships between positive energizers and less ener-gizing people, creating teams including energizers, leading developmental activities to increase the size of the bubbles, and so forth. Knowing who your positive energizers are gives you a distinct advantage.

Activity
Bubble Chart

In your group or organizational unit, ask members to write down the names of three people whom they would rate as the most positive, energizing members. Tabulate the results by identifying the number of nominations received by each person. Create bubbles whose relative sizes represent the number of nominations each person received. There is no special way to arrange the bubbles on the page since their relative sizes provide the most important data.

Once you have developed the bubble chart, consider these questions:

- How many group members received no nominations or were left out? How might they be assisted?
- What is the relationship between hierarchical level in the unit and positive energy? (In some units, some junior-level people are giving energy to the system while some senior-level people are peripheral or are adding little positive energy.)
- Are you thoughtfully managing the energy network in order to capitalize on your positive energizers?

In providing feedback using a bubble chart, be careful that you do not attach names to the bubbles—seeing that one's bubble is very small can cause emotional turmoil or embarrassment. Just use the chart to give people a sense of how the organization is functioning, and then use the data to follow up with individuals who are in need of energy development and with individuals whose energy can be better utilized in the group or organization.

Pulse Survey

A third way to assess energy in your organization is to take a "pulse survey" on a weekly basis, asking employees, "On a 10-point scale, what is the level of your energy today?" Trend lines are tracked and averages are plotted over time for each unit or location. One CEO conducts this survey on a weekly basis and intervenes or provides needed support for units in which positive energy diminishes or in which trend lines turn down.

Activity
Pulse Survey

Use a graph like the one in Figure 11 to keep track of the energy levels of members in your unit over a period of time. Create an average trend line, and where there are significant changes in the trend, either up or down, note what events or incidents occurred around that time. This will help you discover factors that affect energy levels in your organization and identify people who are sources of positive energy as well as who are enablers and disablers of positive energy in the organization.

Now that you have been made aware of the importance of positive energy, you should identify your own key ideas for fostering and unleashing positive energy in your organization. Remember that positive relational energy is primarily a

FIGURE 11

Mapping Energy Via a Pulse Survey

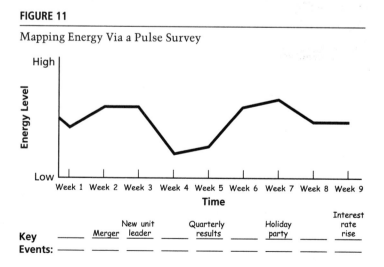

product of flourishing interpersonal relationships and is not the same as mere motivation, incentive systems, or recognition. Positive energy can be taught and learned, and effective positive leaders recognize, reward, and develop positive energizers.

CONCLUSION

Most people easily understand the concept of positive energy, but it is almost never consciously managed in organizations. One reason is that we really have not known how to define or assess it until recently. The scientific research is clear: positive energizers are significantly higher performers than their colleagues, and positive energy is, by a large margin, a more significant factor in the performance of individuals and organizations than people's titles, the information they possess, the influence they exert, or their personality attributes. In my own work, I have found that positive energy is a dramatically underutilized resource and that identifying energy networks and highlighting the major sources of positive energy in an organization have been among the most important ways of improving performance.

In my own academic department at the University of Michigan, positive energy is so important that it is one of the key criteria we use for hiring new faculty members and admitting doctoral students. People have to be net positive energizers—adding more positive energy to the system than they extract—in order to be admitted as members. After twenty years of applying this criterion, it has produced a spectacularly high performing, energizing set of colleagues.

Again, positive energy is primarily a product of flourishing interpersonal relationships and is not the same as motivation, incentive systems, or recognition. Positive energy can be taught and learned, and effective positive leaders recognize, reward, and develop positive energizers.

4
HOW TO DELIVER NEGATIVE FEEDBACK POSITIVELY

As I noted in Chapter 1, positive leadership does not mean constantly smiling, always having sweet interactions, and being perpetually cheerful. The realities of leadership mean that you will sometimes have to deliver messages that are uncomplimentary, negative in tone, or critical of others' performance, and you will have to tackle difficult issues and address challenging problems. This chapter introduces positive leaders to a series of tools and practices that help build and strengthen relationships even though corrective or disapproving feedback must be delivered. The core of this chapter discusses *supportive communication*—practices for being critical without producing defensiveness, bruising others' egos, or invalidating opposing points of view.

THE IMPORTANCE OF FLOURISHING RELATIONSHIPS

As Chapter 3 demonstrated, strong positive relationships do not just occur by chance but are built on positive practices. Moreover, a great deal of research supports the idea that positive interpersonal relationships are a key to creating extraordinarily positive performance in individuals and in organizations.[1] Positive relationships create energy and vitality, which have profound personal impact, including improved health and longer life expectancy. For example, people in positive relationships have less cancer and fewer heart attacks, recover from surgery twice as fast, contract fewer minor illnesses, cope better with stress, have fewer accidents, and have a longer life expectancy than people not in positive relationships.[2, 3]

Not surprisingly, the performance of organizations is also enhanced by the presence of positive relationships among employees. Positive relationships foster cooperation among people, so the things that get in the way of highly successful performance—conflict, disagreements, confusion, ambiguity, unproductive competition, anger, personal offense—are minimized. When positive relationships characterize the workforce, employees are more loyal and committed to their work and to the organization itself, and information exchange, dialogue, and knowledge transfer are significantly enhanced. Creativity and innovation as well as the ability of the system to adapt to change are substantially higher as well.[4]

THE PROBLEM WITH NEGATIVE MESSAGES

Given the importance of positive interpersonal relationships, why are so many relationships problematic? Personality or style differences may create uneasiness, of course, but a major culprit is the difficulty of maintain-

ing strong, positive relationships when there are disagreements, problems, or the need to provide negative
or corrective feedback. Positive leadership practices can
help you strengthen relationships in such situations
rather than have them deteriorate or lead to conflict.

When principles of supportive communication are not
followed, two major obstacles to interpersonal relationships arise: *defensiveness* and *disconfirmation*. In defensiveness, an individual feels threatened or attacked as a
result of a communication. For that person, self-protection
becomes more important than listening. Aggression, anger, competitiveness, or avoidance are common reactions.
Defensiveness may be pervasive within organizations
when people feel punished or inadequately recognized.

Disconfirmation occurs when people feel put down,
ineffectual, or insignificant because of a communication. They feel that their worth as a person or their
competence as a contributor is being questioned or is diminished. As a result, they focus more on building themselves up than on listening. Sometimes people react with
self-aggrandizing or show-off behaviors, or with exagger-
ated self-importance. Alternatively, they may react with
loss of motivation, withdrawal, or loss of respect for the
person delivering the negative message.

When things are going well and people are doing
what you like, it is not difficult to communicate
supportively—to express confidence, trust, and encouragement. But when you have to correct someone else's
behavior, deliver negative feedback, or point out someone's shortcomings, communicating in a way that builds

and strengthens the relationship is more difficult. In order to avoid offending others, most people soft-pedal their negative messages, try to provide hints without directly addressing the issue, or find a way to finesse the communication rather than to be honest, direct, and authentic. The trouble is, with those tactics the issues are rarely resolved, and relationships are seldom strengthened by indirect strategies or soft-pedaling. Addressing negative issues directly and straightforwardly while bolstering the positive relationship is the objective of supportive communication.

ATTRIBUTES OF SUPPORTIVE COMMUNICATION

Interpersonal relationships flourish when they feature more positive communication than negative communication. A variety of studies show that a positive-to-negative ratio of at least three to one, and preferably five to one, is ideal in all types of human relationships.[5] Marriages are stronger, teams are more effective, and organizational performance is higher when there are approximately five positive statements for every negative one.[6]

This is not to say that interpersonal relationships must never include any negative statements, of course. There are always negative elements in any strong relationship, and being inauthentic and insincere by always being complimentary is not helpful. The ideal ratio in flourishing relationships is not five to zero. There are always some negative interchanges in any strong relationship. The question is, how do you handle the one negative in the five-to-one ratio so that the relationship is strengthened? The attributes of supportive communication that we will discuss in this chapter help ensure not only that messages are delivered accurately and straightforwardly but also the relationship between the two parties is supported, even enhanced, by the interchange. People can feel valued, energized, and uplifted even when the information being communicated is negative.

Note also that the goal of supportive communication is not merely to be liked by other people or to be judged a nice person. Rather, positive interpersonal relationships have practical, instrumental value in organizations. Supportive communication, therefore, is not just a "nice-person technique" but a proven competitive advantage for both organizations and their employees.

Supportive Communication Is Congruent, Not Incongruent

Most researchers and observers agree that the best interpersonal communications, and the best relationships, are based on *congruence*. That is, what is communicated, both verbally and nonverbally, matches exactly what the individual is thinking and feeling.[7] Congruence simply means being completely honest. It means communicating what you intend to say. It is synonymous with being authentic, sincere, straightforward, and accurate.

Striving to be honest and open and to demonstrate authenticity does not mean that you blow off steam immediately upon getting upset, nor does it mean that you cannot repress certain inappropriate feelings (e.g., keeping anger, disappointment, or aggression under wraps). Achieving congruence at the expense of all other considerations is not productive. But how do you communicate congruently and straightforwardly without creating defensiveness or disconfirmation? How do you say exactly what you feel without offending the other person? This is where the other three attributes of supportive communication come into play.

Supportive Communication Is Descriptive, Not Evaluative

Among the most important attributes of supportive communication is to be *descriptive* rather than *evaluative* in the delivery of the message.

Evaluation makes a judgment or places a label on other individuals or on their behavior: "You did it wrong." "It's your fault." "You are incompetent." These evaluations generally make other people feel attacked or disconfirmed, and consequently they are likely to react defensively: "I am *not* wrong." "It is not my fault." "*I'm* more capable than *you* are." The end result can be arguments, bad feelings, and a deterioration in the relationship. Self-defensiveness, judgmental statements, and accusations are likely to follow.

The tendency to evaluate others is strongest when the issue is emotionally charged. Sometimes people try to resolve their own bad feelings or anxieties by labeling others. "You are dumb" implies "Therefore, I am smart." Or they may have such strong feelings that they want to punish the other person for violating their expectations or standards: "What you have done deserves to be punished. You have it coming." Most often, however, communications turn into evaluations merely because people do not know how to be congruent without being judgmental.

By contrast, description is the alternative to evaluation.[8] Descriptive communication allows a person to be congruent and authentic as well as helpful. This type of communication involves three steps:

1. Describe the event, behavior, or circumstance objectively.
2. Describe outcomes and/or your feelings, not the other person's attributes.
3. Suggest alternative solutions that could resolve the issue.

First, *describe objectively your observation of the event that occurred or the behavior that you think needs to be modified.* As dispassionately as possible, talk about what happened instead of the person involved: "You just interrupted me for the second time." "Your assignment was not in on time." If possible, this description should identify elements of the behavior that can be confirmed objectively. Compare the behavior to an accepted standard rather than to a personal opinion or preference. Avoid talking about what you think the other person's motives were. Approaching the matter in this way makes it less likely that the other person will feel attacked or unfairly treated, since no evaluative label is being placed on him or her. A descriptive statement is as objective and verifiable as possible.

Second, *describe your (or others') reactions to the behavior or describe the consequences of the behavior.* Avoid projecting the cause of the problem onto the other person. This requires you to be aware of your own reactions and able to describe them: "I get frustrated when I cannot finish my thought." "I am concerned about the effects on the team's performance." Or the consequences of the behavior can be pointed out: "The issue is not getting clarified." "Department members are complaining." Describing feelings or consequences lessens the likelihood of defensiveness since the problem is framed in the context of your feelings or the objective consequences, not the attributes of the other person. If those feelings or consequences are described in a non-accusing way, the major energies of the communicators can be focused on problem solving rather than on defending against evaluations.

Third, *suggest a more acceptable alternative.* This focuses the discussion on alternative solutions, not on the person. It avoids accusations. It also helps the other person save face and avoid feeling personally criticized because the behavior is separated from self-worth. "I promise to give you time to make your points if you will let me finish mine." "What if I send you a reminder a couple of days before the deadline?" Such a discussion preserves self-esteem because it focuses on something that is controllable and on which the two parties can agree. Of course, take care not to make the problem entirely the other person's responsibility to resolve: "I don't like the way things are. What are *you* going to do about it?" The change need not be the responsibility of only one of the communicating parties. Instead, the emphasis should be on finding a solution that is acceptable to both people, not on deciding who is right and who is wrong, or who should change and who should not.

To sum up the three steps of descriptive communication: (1) "Here is what I just experienced," (2) "Here is how I feel about it, or here are the consequences," and (3) "Here is an alternative that would be more acceptable."

One concern regarding descriptive communication is that these steps may not work unless the other person also knows the rules of supportive communication. Otherwise, the person who does not want to be supportive can subvert any positive result. The other person might simply reply: "I don't care how you feel." Or "I have an excuse for what happened, so it's not my fault." Or "It's too bad if this annoys you. It's your problem."

How might you deal with these responses? Do you abandon principles of descriptive communication and become evaluative and defensive in return? Do you engage in the "Yes, you are," "No, I'm not," "Yes, you are," "No, I'm not" kind of argument? Do you just write off the other person as being incorrigible?

The prescription is not to abandon the three steps of descriptive communication. Rather, focus on the other person's lack of concern or defensive reaction as the priority problem. For example, the problem of frequent interruptions will be very difficult to address as long as the more important interpersonal problem is blocking progress. In effect, the focus must shift from interruptions to the expressed attitude or the fundamental obstacle that inhibits working together to improve performance. Effective supportive communicators do not abandon the three steps. They simply switch the focus. They might respond, "I'm surprised to hear you say that you don't care how I feel about this problem [step 1]. Your response concerns me, and I think it might have important implications for the productivity of our team [step 2]. I suggest we spend some time trying to identify the obstacles you feel might be inhibiting our ability to work together on this problem [step 3]."

When it is necessary to make evaluative statements, the evaluations should be made in terms of some established criteria (e.g., "Your behavior does not meet the prescribed standard"), some probable outcomes (e.g., "Continuation of your behavior will lead to worse consequences"), or some past successes by the same individual (e.g., "This behavior is not as good as your past behavior"). The important point is to avoid disconfirming the other person or arousing defensiveness.

Supportive Communication Is
Problem-Oriented, Not Person-Oriented

Problem-oriented communication focuses on problems and solutions rather than on personal traits: "This is the problem." By contrast, *person-oriented* communication focuses on the characteristics of the individual, not the event: "You are the problem." Problem-oriented communication is useful even when personal appraisals are called for because it focuses on behaviors, events, and standards. Person-oriented communication, on the other hand, often focuses on things that seldom can be changed or controlled, and it can send the message that the individual is simply inadequate. A good rule of thumb is to avoid using the word "you" in providing feedback. Instead, target the behavior, the event, the consequences, and the standard that has not been met.

In building positive, supportive relationships, problem-oriented communication should always be linked to accepted standards or expectations rather than to personal opinions. An opinion is more likely to be interpreted as person-oriented and arouse defensiveness than a statement in which the behavior is compared to an accepted standard of performance.

Supportive Communication Validates Rather Than Invalidates Individuals

Communication that is *invalidating* arouses negative feelings about self-worth, identity, and relatedness to others. It denies the presence, uniqueness, or importance of another individual. Especially damaging are communications that invalidate people by conveying superiority, rigidity, indifference, and imperviousness.

Communication that is superiority oriented gives the impression that the communicator is informed whereas others are ignorant, adequate whereas others are inadequate, competent whereas others are incompetent, or powerful whereas others are impotent. Rigidity is communicated when one person's point of view is portrayed as absolute, unequivocal, or unquestionable; no other opinion or point of view could possibly be considered to be legitimate. Indifference is communicated when the other person's existence or importance is not acknowledged: by refusing to respond to the other person's statements, by avoiding eye contact, by interrupting the other person frequently, by using impersonal words ("people think that . . ." instead of "I think that . . ."), or by engaging in unrelated activity during a conversation. Imperviousness means that the communicator dismisses or denigrates the feelings or opinions of the other person, labeling him or her as either illegitimate ("You shouldn't feel that way," "Your opinion is incorrect,") or ignorant ("You don't understand," "You've been misinformed," "Your opinion is naive"). All of these invalidating practices exclude the other person's contribution to the conversation or the relationship and make the other person feel inconsequential and unimportant.

Validating communication, on the other hand, helps people feel recognized, understood, accepted, and valued. It has four attributes: it is respectful, flexible, two-way, and based on agreement.

Respectful communicators help others feel that they have a stake in identifying problems and resolving concerns by communicating an egalitarian stance. They treat others as worthwhile, competent, and insightful, and they emphasize mutual problem solving rather than projecting a superior position. They can do this merely by asking questions—that is, by seeking the opinions, suggestions, and ideas of the other person. Research has confirmed that asking questions is more likely to result in a productive relationship than is declaring or advocating a point of view.[9] Flexibility in communication is the willingness of one person to acknowledge that the other party may possess additional data or be aware of other alternatives that could make important contributions both to the problem solution and to the relationship. It simply indicates being receptive to the other person's perspective. It is the opposite of being dogmatic and unwilling to listen. Two-way communication is an implied result of respectfulness and flexibility. Individuals feel validated when they are asked questions, given airtime to express their opinions, and encouraged to participate actively in the interpersonal interaction. Two-way interchange communicates the message that the other person is valued and that there is genuine interest in his or her perspective. It is a prerequisite for building collaboration and teamwork. One rule of thumb for enhancing two-way interchange is to make certain that one person speaks no more than three or four sentences before giving the other person a chance to communicate.

Validation also occurs when the communicator attempts to identify areas of agreement or areas of joint commitment. Almost all models of negotiation, team building, and conflict resolution prescribe finding something upon which both parties can agree.[10] Agreement makes progress possible. Therefore, communicators should keep in mind the question "On what do we agree?" and verbalize that common agreement periodically in the exchange.

Being positive is not always possible, of course, and all flourishing relationships—and organizations—face trials, challenges, and negative events. To help turn these circumstances into relationship-strengthening interactions, these principles of supportive communication can help.

Supportive Communication: Summary

Congruence: Be authentic, sincere, straightforward, and honest in delivering communication.

Description: Objectively describe events, describe reactions or consequences, suggest alternatives.

Problem focus: Focus on the problem rather than the person's shortcomings.

Respect: Communicate respect for the other person's point of view.

Inquiry: Ask as much as you declare. Ask questions first.

Common agreement: Identify and reiterate areas of shared agreement.

Positive ratios: Use at least three, and ideally five, positive statements for every negative statement.

Two-way: Say only three or four sentences before you give the other person a chance to speak.

In order to become competent at supportive communication, people need to practice doing it. Knowing how to communicate supportively is not an inherent attribute or personality characteristic. Rather, it is a skill that positive leaders can develop. The following three exercises are designed to help you practice and enhance your competency in using supportive communication.

Activity
Practice and Gather Feedback

Hold a ten- or fifteen-minute conversation with a colleague who possesses a different point of view about any of the topics in the list below (or one of your own choice).

- Should the United States engage in nation building outside its own borders?
- Should late-term abortions be performed?
- Is global warming primarily affected by human behavior?
- Should the United States provide free public education and health care for illegal aliens?
- Should people be allowed to be publicly critical of Muhammad, Jesus, or Buddha?
- Should China be allowed to censor Google and Facebook?
- Are school and university rankings in magazines helpful or harmful?
- Is a postgraduate degree worth the money?
- Who is the world's most dangerous person?
- Should the United Nations exist?

Take a position on the issue and make a case for your point of view. Your job is to convince your partner that you are correct. Your partner's job is to convince you that the opposite point of view is correct.

When you are finished, rate your colleague on the following items, and have your colleague rate you. Use the following scale: 1 = strongly disagree, 2 = disagree, 3 = neither disagree nor agree, 4 = agree, 5 = strongly agree.

1. Maintained eye contact and expressed interest in my comments.   1 2 3 4 5 NA
2. Used inquiry (asked questions) as much as advocacy (made declarations).   1 2 3 4 5 NA
3. Did not interrupt me before I finished my comments.   1 2 3 4 5 NA
4. Was authentic, congruent, and straightforward.   1 2 3 4 5 NA
5. Used descriptive rather than evaluative statements.   1 2 3 4 5 NA
6. Communicated respect for the opposing viewpoint.   1 2 3 4 5 NA
7. Periodically identified areas of common agreement.   1 2 3 4 5 NA
8. Used three to five positive statements for every negative statement.   1 2 3 4 5 NA
9. Focused on the problem rather than my personal attributes.   1 2 3 4 5 NA
10. Made only three or four statements before allowing me to speak.   1 2 3 4 5 NA

Total Score: _____

Based on the scores your colleague gave you on the questionnaire, in what areas do you need the most improvement?

_____

Activity
Earn the Right to Reply

This exercise is designed to help you practice your ability to genuinely listen and to communicate respect for the point of view of the other person.

Choose a discussion topic from the list in the exercise above (or another topic of your choice), hold a conversation with a person who possesses an opposing point of view. Determine by the flip of a coin which partner will speak first. In order to earn the right to reply, partner 2 must repeat to the satisfaction of partner 1 the essence of the message that partner 1 just delivered. This is not a matter of regurgitating word for word what partner 1 said. Rather, partner 2 must repeat the general message that partner 1 communicated, and partner 1 must agree that his or her message was accurately understood. If partner 1 does not feel that partner 2 has reflected the message accurately, partner 1 should help clarify the message so that it is understood accurately. Once agreement has been reached, then partner 2 has a chance to present his or her point of view. In order to earn the right to reply, partner 1 must now summarize the message to the satisfaction of partner 2. This process is repeated for as long as the conversation lasts.

At the end of the conversation, respond to these questions, and discuss your answers with your partner.

1. How easy was it for you to accurately reflect the messages of your partner?
2. Did summarizing your partner's point of view help you be more respectful of your partner and more descriptive in your replies?

3. Did your points of view move closer together or further apart as the conversation progressed?
4. What was the most frustrating part of this exercise?
5. What was the most enjoyable part of this exercise?

Activity
Provide Feedback

This exercise is designed to help you practice providing non-positive feedback to another person using supportive communication. The exercise must be completed with a person you know reasonably well—a spouse, close colleague, or friend.

Read the following questions and write down your answer to each as it applies to your partner. Be as accurate, direct, and straightforward as you can in your written response.

1. Here is what I admire about you.
2. Here is what I consider to be your greatest strengths and unique capabilities.
3. If you are to achieve your maximum potential, here is what I think you need to improve.

Using your written answers as notes or reminders, provide this information verbally to your partner. Address each of the items separately.

After you have finished, ask your partner to answer the following questions about your communication. (In order for your partner to be able to accurately rate your communication, you may need to explain each of these dimensions to him or her. Teaching your partner about the principles of supportive communication is an effective way to learn and practice it yourself.) Ask for feedback about the extent to which you were effective in utilizing supportive communication. Use the following response scale: 1 = strongly disagree, 2 = disagree, 3 = neither disagree nor agree, 4 = agree, 5 = strongly agree.

1. Used inquiry (asked questions) as much as advocacy (made declarations).   1 2 3 4 5 NA
2. Displayed congruence (authenticity and straightforwardness).   1 2 3 4 5 NA
3. Used descriptive rather than evaluative statements.   1 2 3 4 5 NA
4. Communicated respect for the opposing viewpoint.   1 2 3 4 5 NA
5. Periodically identified areas of common agreement.   1 2 3 4 5 NA
6. Used three to five positive statements for every negative statement.   1 2 3 4 5 NA
7. Focused on controllable behaviors rather than on personal attributes.   1 2 3 4 5 NA
8. Made only three or four statements before allowing me to speak.   1 2 3 4 5 NA

Discuss the ratings given to you by your partner. In what areas do you need practice and development? In what areas are you especially skilled and effective?

CONCLUSION

This chapter's purpose is to help you successfully handle difficult, uncomfortable, potentially explosive interactions. You can still be a positive leader in those circumstances if you use the steps of supportive communication. These techniques—avoiding defensiveness and disconfirmation, demonstrating congruence, using descriptive statements, making problem-oriented statements, and validating the other person—are proven ways to build strong relationships even in the face of disagreements.

5
HOW TO ESTABLISH AND ACHIEVE EVEREST GOALS

Climbing Mt. Everest is among the most challenging activities most people can imagine. It requires supreme planning, training, effort, teamwork, and personal mastery. Very few of us have the physical, mental, and emotional capability to even attempt this level of performance. In organizations, Everest goals share similar attributes—they represent the peak, the culmination, the supreme achievement that we can imagine. They represent accomplishment well beyond ordinary success. But Everest goals are not just fantasies or dreams. They possess special attributes that actually motivate spectacular performance.

Everest goals have been found to help people accomplish outcomes that they never expected to accomplish, and they have helped organizations reach levels of performance previously unimagined.[1] This chapter will help you begin the process of identifying an Everest goal for yourself and/or for your organization and assist you in developing a strategy for reaching the goal.

The first step in understanding the role of Everest goals is to understand the importance of goals and goal setting in individual and organizational performance. The chapter helps you identify the extent to which you recognize and utilize effective goals in your own life, and then the unique attributes of Everest goals are explained. Application activities will help you begin the process of establishing an Everest goal for yourself and/ or for your organization.

THE IMPORTANCE OF GOALS

A great deal of research confirms that having goals motivates individuals and organizations to achieve higher performance than if they have no goals.[2] For example, if you are assigned a task but are given no targets or standards for performance, you are unlikely to perform as well as if you are clear about the objective and the level of performance expected of you. Goal setting is a common strategy for helping individuals improve their performance. If we want high performance, we almost always establish goals as a way to attain it.[3]

In organizations, the situation is the same. Organizational performance is reliably predicted by the extent to which goals have been established. It is common in organizations, for example, for leaders to establish company goals for the year, goals for each subunit, annual goals for every employee, and long-term goals targeting several years into the future. Goals for motivating performance in organizations are almost universal.

TYPES OF GOALS

The kinds of goals established are important in predicting success. Figure 12 illustrates some of the effects of different types of goals on performance.[4]

Easy goals: If you are told that most people accomplish ten tasks per day but, because you are such a valuable employee, it is okay if you accomplish five tasks, you will most likely accomplish a number closer to five than to ten. Your performance will not be high with an easy goal.

General goals: If you are given a general goal such as "Do your best" or "Just work hard," your performance will be higher than if you are given an easy goal. You will not likely slack off, but you will probably not achieve at the highest levels of your potential either.

FIGURE 12

Goal Setting and Performance

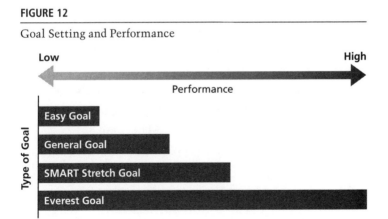

Stretch goals and SMART stretch goals: If you are told that you are such a valuable employee that you are sure to exceed the average of ten tasks a day and are given the goal of accomplishing fifteen tasks a day, it is likely that you will achieve a level of performance closer to fifteen tasks than to ten. Stretch goals are especially effective in influencing performance if they have five attributes characterized by the acronym SMART:

- *S = Specific* (versus general). A specific goal provides a clear standard or level of performance. Specific goals are precise, detailed, and explicit, and they are more likely to be achieved than general goals. For example: "Our goal is 95 percent customer satisfaction" rather than "Our goal is to have satisfied customers."
- *M = Measurable* (versus vague). A measurable goal can be clearly assessed and quantified. Being able to measure goal achievement increases the likelihood that it will be achieved. For example: "Our goal is to win twenty games this season" rather than "Our goal is to have a successful season."
- *A = Aligned* (versus unrelated). Aligned goals are consistent with the purposes of the organization. Aligned goals are more achievable because they engender support from others in the organization compared to goals that have little relationship to what the organization cares about. When it comes to

individuals, such goals are aligned with core values, helping a person make progress on things he or she cares deeply about. For example: "Our goal is to donate ten hours per week for tutoring at-risk children" rather than "Our goal is to give time to community service."

- *R = Realistic* (versus impossible to attain). A realistic goal should be difficult—that is, create stretch—but not impossible. Becoming an Olympic athlete by next month, for example, is not realistic for most people. Realistic goals are achievable rather than being merely fantasies or dreams. For example: "Our goal is to conduct at least one food drive every six months" rather than "Our goal is to wipe out poverty in Detroit."

- *T = Time-bound* (versus limitless). A time-bound goal identifies a deadline for when the goal will have been achieved. Limitless goals can go on indefinitely with no real sense of whether the goal has been achieved or not. For example: "Our goal is to generate revenues of $15 million by the end of the fiscal year" rather than "Our goal is to reach a $15 million plateau."

Activity
SMART Goals

Write down one goal that you have for your work, your personal life, or your family. Now, using the rating scale below, analyze your goal statement in terms of the extent to which it is a SMART stretch goal.

The goal is specific	Absolutely	Unsure	Probably not
The goal is measurable	Absolutely	Unsure	Probably not
The goal is aligned	Absolutely	Unsure	Probably not
The goal is realistic	Absolutely	Unsure	Probably not
The goal is time-bound	Absolutely	Unsure	Probably not
The goal is a stretch	Absolutely	Unsure	Probably not

For a work-related goal, this activity is even more effective if you have a colleague who will rate your goal. Consider having everyone in your organization share and evaluate goals. That way, colleagues can provide suggestions for improvement to one another regarding the extent to which the goals are SMART stretch goals.

EVEREST GOALS

Everest goals represent a special kind of goals. While they usually have the attributes of SMART stretch goals, they also possess five unique attributes. They:

1. Are positively deviant
2. Represent goods of first intent
3. Possess an affirmative orientation
4. Represent a contribution
5. Create and foster sustainable positive energy

Everest Goals Represent Positive Deviance

In English, the term *deviance* usually has a negative connotation. When we label someone a "deviant," it is usually a criticism. Yet *deviance* merely refers to a condition that is not normal—an aberration from the standard or something that is unexpected.

We can think, therefore, of *negative deviance*, but we can also think of *positive deviance*. To illustrate what positive deviance means, consider the continuum in Figure 13. A condition of negative deviance (represented by mistakes and errors) is represented on the left, a normal or expected condition is in the center, and a positively deviant or extraordinarily desirable condition is shown on the right. The right-hand point on the continuum can also be referred to as a *virtuous state*— meaning the best of the human condition or the highest aspirations that human beings hold for themselves.

An obvious example might be physical health. The large majority of medical research, and almost all of

FIGURE 13

A Deviance Continuum

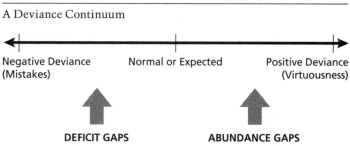

medical professionals' time, is spent somewhere between the left point on the continuum (illness or injury) and the middle point (the normal condition of health), which is defined as an absence of illness or injury. Relatively little scientific attention is given to the gap between normal physical health (the middle point) and extraordinary vitality or, for example, Olympic-level fitness (the right-hand point). The right-hand end of the continuum represents a condition of positively deviant health. Scientifically, we know much less about positively deviant physical health than we do about illness.[5]

The space between the left-hand side of the continuum and the middle can be called the *deficit gap*, where there are problems, obstacles, and mistakes. The space between the middle point and the right-hand side can be called the *abundance gap*. Everest goals focus on the abundance gap rather than the deficit gap. They aim not just to overcome problems and achieve success but to reach extraordinarily high levels of performance—performance that spectacularly and dramatically exceeds normal.[6] In this they are similar to an abundance culture in organizations by reaching for the highest aspirations of humankind.

Everest Goals Represent Goods of First Intent

Everest goals are also virtuous, focusing on achieving the best of the human condition, in that they are similar to what the Greek philosopher Aristotle called "goods of first intent." Goods of first intent, he proposed, represent that which "is good in itself and is to be chosen for its own sake," such as love, wisdom, and fulfillment.[7] Goods of first intent possess inherent value and are desirable because of intrinsic value. On the other hand, goods of second intent include "that which is good for the sake of obtaining something else," such as profit, prestige, or power.[8] One indicator of the difference between goods of first intent and goods of second intent is that people never tire of or become satiated with goods of first intent. It is not possible to get too much of a good of first intent, such as love or wisdom. This is not true of goods of second intent which can lead to satiation and diminishing returns.

Like Aristotle's goods of first intent, Everest goals possess inherent meaning and purpose. With an Everest goal, achieving the outcome itself is sufficient; the goal is not a means to obtain another end, such as recognition, reward, or acclaim. The achievement of the Everest goal itself possesses all the value and significance that we need.[9] This is very much akin to feeling a sense of *calling* in work.[10]

Everest Goals Possess an Affirmative Orientation

An affirmative orientation refers to an inclination toward positive possibilities—toward "Why not?" rather than "Why?" Everest goals do not merely focus on solving problems, reducing obstacles, overcoming challenges, or removing difficulties. Rather, Everest goals focus on opportunities, possibilities, and potential. Everest goals are more likely to emphasize strengths and capitalize on gifts than address weaknesses and past failures. They affirm an optimistic orientation. They do not merely eliminate problems. With an Everest goal, virtuousness is the desired outcome.[11]

Everest Goals Represent a Contribution

The achievement of a goal can be thought to provide benefits or rewards either to the person pursuing the goal or to others. Thus, goals can be categorized as *achievement goals* (when they benefit the person pursuing the goal) or as *contribution goals* (when they benefit others). Most people pursue both kinds of goals, but one or the other type usually predominates in people and in organizations.

Achievement goals emphasize self-interest, achieving desired outcomes, obtaining a preferred reward, accomplishing something that brings self-satisfaction or enhances self-esteem, and creates a positive image in the eyes of others. Individuals who emphasize achievement goals are primarily interested in proving themselves, reinforcing self-worth, or demonstrating competency. Attaining desired performance outcomes is the primary objective.

Contribution goals focus on providing benefit to others. These goals emphasize what individuals can give compared to what they can get. Contribution goals are motivated more by benevolence than by a desire for acquisition.

Jennifer Crocker and her colleagues found that goals focused on contributing to others produced a *growth* orientation in individuals over time, whereas self-interest goals produced a *proving* orientation over time. In studies of individuals tracked over several months,

Crocker found that contribution goals led to significantly more learning and development, higher levels of interpersonal trust, relationships that were more supportive, higher performance, and less depression and loneliness than did self-interest goals. Most important, when contribution goals predominated, the meaningfulness of activities was substantially higher than when self-interested goals predominated.[12]

Everest goals focus on contributions rather than personal benefits, the creation of value rather than personal payback, and ensuring value for others rather than acquisition for oneself. Contribution goals enable the best of the human condition.

Everest Goals Foster Sustainable Positive Energy

As Chapter 3 mentions, there are several kinds of human energy: physical, emotional, and relational. Of the three types, only relational energy is renewed with use rather than exhausted, and this is why it is associated with positive, supportive relationships. Positively energizing relationships are *amplifying* in that they create additional energy the more they are used. Loving, caring relationships are renewed the more we engage in them. Moreover, this form of energy is its own reward. People do not pursue relational energy in order to obtain another, more important outcome. It is sufficient in itself.

Similarly, Everest goals are inherently energizing. We are not exhausted by pursuing Everest goals; instead we are uplifted, elevated, and energized. Nor do we need another source of motivation to pursue them: the goal itself provides the necessary positive energy for its pursuit. Ed Deci's concept of intrinsic motivation shares a similar connotation.[13]

Everest goals are not the same as personal mission statements, life purpose statements, or statements of what we stand for. Everest goals are also not the same as an organization's core competencies, a corporate vision statement, or a strategic plan. Such philosophical statements differ from Everest goals because they do not have the five SMART attributes. Everest goals are, first and foremost, *goals*—they drive behavior.[14]

AN EXAMPLE OF AN ORGANIZATIONAL EVEREST GOAL

Everest goals are difficult to develop—they usually cannot be developed off the top of the head or after superficial consideration. In fact, most individuals and organizations have never developed these kinds of goals for themselves. Although there is no boilerplate way to determine appropriate Everest goals, it may help to have some examples of Everest goals established by organizations that produced dramatic improvement.

For example, in 1951 the U.S. government established a facility in Colorado to produce the triggers used in the nuclear weapons stockpiled during the Cold War. At the end of the Cold War, the U.S. Department of Energy mandated that the site—labeled by ABC News as the most dangerous place in America due to the amount of radioactive and explosive materials stored on the site, including plutonium, enriched uranium, and dangerous chemicals—be closed and cleaned up. A blue-ribbon panel of experts from around the globe conducted a study to determine how long the cleanup would take and how much it would cost. The most optimistic estimate was seventy years at a cost of $36 billion, although the more realistic estimate was two hundred years and several hundred billion dollars.

The company that won the contract established the following Everest goal—thought at the time by the Department of Energy, the Government Accountability Office, and the other nuclear facilities throughout the country to be delusional: "We will clean up and close the facility in twelve years in order to remove as quickly as possible, and forever, the threat of personal harm, pollution, and the dangers of radioactivity for our children and grandchildren." The consequence of establishing that goal was that the cleanup and closure actually took only ten years at a cost of $6 billion, and it left the site thirteen times cleaner than required by federal standards.[15] Let us highlight this goal's Everest attributes.

- The original goal of twelve years was *positively deviant*, as experts considered that time frame to be fantasy.
- The driving motive of the goal, to make the world safe for future generations, was a *good of first intent*. No more important outcome was needed.
- The goal focused on positive possibilities—to exceed all realistic estimations—despite pervasive opposition from others. Thus, it had an *affirmative orientation*.

- Workers were making a *contribution* to others and to future generations. Furthermore, they were willing to sacrifice, for others' benefit, the extra money they could have earned by stretching out the job.

- The challenge created *sustainable positive energy*, engendering passion and complete dedication in employees, even to the extent of enthusiastically giving up their jobs.

Another example is the Everest goal established in 2005 by the leadership team at one of the Prudential Financial Services companies. The pressure on this firm from Wall Street to achieve financial success was tremendous. The initial goal, therefore, was stated in financial terms: "We want to earn $10 million in profits by 2010"—at the time an almost impossible goal.

However, after learning about the concept of Everest goals, the leadership team decided to change the wording of the goal. Leaders recognized that few employees get up each morning energized by and passionate about earning $10 million in profits. The goal was altered, therefore, to better reflect the attributes of Everest goals: "We will ensure that ten million people will have secure retirement by the year 2010." Given performance trends current at the time, this goal represented a *positively deviant* target in everyone's minds. Now employees could imagine their grandparents being assured of a reasonable quality of life in retirement: a *good of first intent*. They could imagine an elderly friend whose medical care was ensured because of the company's commitment, giving the goal an *affirmative orientation*. They could envision making a *contribution* to people they would never meet but whose lives would be better because of their success. And the *sustainable positive energy* that was generated by this goal led to extraordinarily high performance levels. The trajectory of the firm's performance changed markedly after its goal became Everest-like.

Other examples of company Everest goals include the following:

- Ford Motor Company: democratize the automobile (early 1900s)
- Boeing: bring the world into the jet age (1950s)
- Sony: change the image of poor quality in Japanese products (1960s)
- Apple: one person, one computer (1980s)

An example of an Everest goal in business that is outside the framework of a single company is the C. K. Prahalad Initiative, which seeks to reframe the way businesses deal with the world's poorest inhabitants. It asserts that companies can "tap new markets while solving some social problems and empowering the estimated four billion people living on less than $2 a day."[16] Here the goal is to have half a million Indians become employable within ten years.

Everest goals are not the same as mere stretch goals, in that they extend beyond them. Sometimes SMART stretch goals share some of the attributes of Everest goals (most particularly the emphasis on positive deviance), but usually they are lacking some or all of the other four (good of first intent, affirmative orientation, contribution, and sustainable positive energy). You can see the differences when you look at some of the following company stretch goals from the past fifty years that are not Everest goals: GE's "Be #1 or #2 in every market we serve," Walmart's "Become the first trillion-dollar company," Philip Morris's "Knock off RJR as the #1 tobacco company," Nike's "Crush Adidas," Honda's "Destroy Yamaha," and Giro Sport's "Become the Nike of the cycling industry" (which, incidentally, built on Nike's success at its own stretch goal from several decades earlier).

AN EXAMPLE OF AN EVEREST GOAL FOR INDIVIDUALS

Individuals may also identify and pursue personal Everest goals on their own. These have the same attributes discussed above: the same standard of positive deviance, the same inherent meaningfulness, the same affirmative orientation, the same focus on contribution, the same positive energy. Identifying an Everest goal can allow a person to do something he or she would normally consider to be impossible.

One example is Rick Hoyt, then a wheelchair-bound student at South Middle School in Westfield, Massachusetts, due to cerebral palsy. Rick came home from watching a high school basketball game one day and told his father—with the help of a head switch atop his wheelchair—about a charity road race staged to benefit a fellow student who was paralyzed in an auto accident. Rick told his father he wanted to be a part of the race. Dick Hoyt decided to establish an Everest goal. Never mind that he was 40 years old and ran just once a week. Never mind that he only ran a mile at a time, at most. Never mind that he was not only being asked to run five miles but to push his son and a 50 pound wheelchair with him. His son wanted to be a part of this race. That is how the Everest goal got set. Since then, Rick and Dick Hoyt have completed 50 marathons and 121 triathlons. They also crossed the country on a bicycle, completing the 3,700 mile trek in 45 days. Importantly, a key objective of the Everest goal was to break down barriers regarding people with disabilities and to teach people about Everest goals. Everest goal achieved.

Activity
Personal Everest Goal

The questions below are intended to help you clarify and pinpoint an Everest goal for your own life. This is not a personal mission statement or a philosophy of life. Because it is an Everest goal, it has SMART attributes—something that can motivate behavior.

Such a goal may relate to your role at work, your life outside of work, your relationships, or something very personal within you. Do not be frustrated or disappointed if nothing comes immediately to mind. Many people have never identified such a goal for themselves, and it is not a quick and easy task to identify an Everest goal that is real and that is meaningful to you. Sometimes this task takes a great deal of contemplation, feedback, and self-analysis, but the outcomes are worth the effort.

- What represents positively deviant performance—significantly above the norm—for you?
- What do you consider an inherently valuable accomplishment, even if no other benefit accrues to you?
- Are you focusing on an affirmative orientation—on positive possibilities—rather than on solving a problem, on abundance rather than overcoming a deficit?
- What contribution will you make to others by achieving this goal?
- Does the goal provide you with energy, enthusiasm, and excitement even if you have no other incentives besides the goal itself?
- In an area about which you care deeply, what is the best performance you can imagine?
- For what do you have passionate commitment and a willingness to put forth full effort to achieve it?
- Do you have a support system that can assist you with your goal accomplishment?

Activity
Organizational Everest Goal

Everest goals are intended to push individuals and organizations to their ultimate limits. Achieving Everest goals in organizations creates spectacularly positive outcomes, but no organization becomes extraordinary by chance. Either a conscious decision is made to pursue an Everest goal or positively deviant performance is unlikely.

Of course, establishing organizational Everest goals is best performed in collaboration with members of your organization. Any attempt to simply superimpose an Everest goal on an organization is doomed to failure. This is because the attributes of Everest goals must be clarified, approved, and shared among those who will be accountable for the organization's performance.

Coming up with an organizational Everest goal will take multiple meetings and intensive discussions among the relevant constituencies. Considering the following questions, however, will give you a head start on that process.

- What achievement represents the culmination—the very best—our organization can be?
- What would create passion among employees?
- What does our organization care deeply about?
- What represents our organization's ultimate destiny?
- What legacy would we like our organization to leave?
- What human benefits do we want to produce?
- What core values and virtues do we represent?
- How can we have an impact that extends beyond immediate outcomes?
- What ripple effects can we create?
- What do our customers or clients care deeply about?
- What outcome is more important than the organization's success?
- What is the best possible outcome we can imagine?

ACHIEVING EVEREST GOALS

Merely establishing an Everest goal is no guarantee that performance will change in any way, of course. Goal statements must be accompanied by additional assistance. Specifically, the goal must be integrated with a set of action steps and accountability mechanisms.

Some years ago, before gastric bypass surgery was invented, a young woman became so depressed that she made the decision to commit suicide. She wanted nothing more than to be married and have children, but she weighed more than four hundred pounds, and she felt that, given her size, it was highly unlikely that she would find a marriage partner and be healthy enough to have children. She had tried stretch goals, SMART goals, incentive systems, therapy, and a host of fad diets to try to change her size, but nothing worked. Finally, in a tremendous amount of emotional and psychological pain, she decided to give up.

Before she was able to put her suicide plan into action, however, she became aware of the concept of Everest goals. With the assistance of a coach and counselor, she decided to see if this tool could help her. The Everest goal she established was to lose a hundred pounds in the next twelve months. Now, this might ordinarily be labeled as merely a SMART stretch goal, but she had been living with those kinds of goals for many years without any progress. For her, only when the goal of losing weight was consciously attached to the five attributes of Everest goals did it change in its character. Such a large weight loss in such a short time was obviously a positively deviant goal, but she also found ways to associate the goal with a good of first intent, an affirmative orientation rather than merely a problem-solving approach, a contribution rather than the pursuit of purely personal benefits, and a source of sustainable positive energy rather than a tortuous journey. The goal took on a much broader meaning than simply to become physically smaller.

She checked with a physician to ensure that this would not be dangerous to her health, and she garnered the assistance of a large social support network to assist her. It was not enough for this network of supporters to merely cheer her on, give her moral support, and be there for her. She already had moral support and friendships, and those had not been enough for her to accomplish an Everest goal.

Instead, she put the following process into place as summarized in Figure 14:

1. Set an Everest goal
2. Identify multiple specific actions
3. Make it more difficult to fail than to succeed
4. Determine effects

The first step, of course, is to establish an Everest goal. But to achieve that goal, three more steps are crucial. The second step involves identifying multiple, specific action steps. The principle is that *the more difficult the goal, the more numerous and more specific the action steps must be.* For example, this young woman determined that she would not shop for food alone, and she

FIGURE 14

Achieving Everest Goals

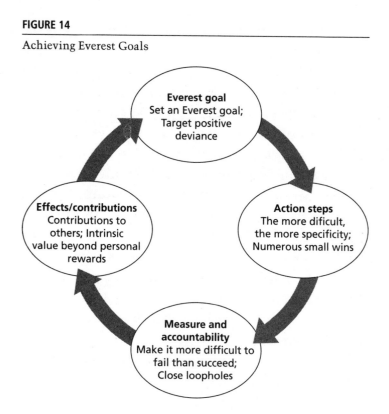

would not shop without a menu. She would meet a friend each morning before work to go to an exercise class. She would carry only enough money in her purse for bus fare, not enough for a hamburger or a bag of donuts. Someone would eat lunch with her each day to ensure that she kept to her targets for portion control. She would only watch television while walking on a treadmill. And, she regularly attended support group meetings. These were just a few of her action steps—the list came to more than twenty. This meant that by the end of each day, she had achieved numerous small victories. These small wins, rather than failures and embarrassments, began to dominate her life. The victories contributed to sustainable positive energy.

The third step, making it more difficult to fail than to succeed, is important because when most of us face a challenge to reach positive deviance, we frequently figure out loopholes that allow us to avoid having to really accomplish the goal. This step closes those loopholes. The young woman in the example took measures that made it more difficult to stay the same weight than to lose weight. Activities included a contract with her supervisor at work to cut her salary in 10 percent increments if she did not achieve weight loss benchmarks; scheduling public weigh-ins at work; an agreement that if she did not lose the weight by the end of the year, her physician would hospitalize her and put her on an intravenous diet until she lost the weight—at a cost to her of $400 per day; and many other activities. She had at least a dozen similar accountability mechanisms, all designed to make it more expensive, more embarrassing, and more difficult to fail than to succeed. This meant that she had both positive incentives and the threat of negative incentives associated with the pursuit of her goal.

The fourth step emphasizes the contribution and the intrinsic motivation associated with the Everest goal. As explained earlier, contribution goals produce more success than achievement goals, and the inherent meaningfulness of the activity produces the positive energy necessary to follow through. For the young woman in the example, staying alive trumped all other outcomes, but that is not all. She turned her attention to contributing to the welfare of others, investing in inherently meaningful activities, and focusing on the long-term, multigenerational effects of her actions.

Did she succeed? Not only did she lose a hundred pounds in twelve months, she went on to eventually lose more than 50 percent of her starting weight.

Activity
Action Steps and Accountability

For either your personal Everest goal or your organizational Everest goal, write down several specific action steps (with corresponding small wins) and the accountability mechanisms (measures, metrics, milestones) you can put into place to help ensure progress toward your Everest goal.

CONCLUSION

Goal setting is a common technique for motivating performance and for maintaining accountability, but as this chapter has highlighted, there are differences between normal goals and Everest goals. Everest goals possess the same attributes as SMART goals—they are specific, measurable, aligned, realistic, and time-bound—but Everest goals possess five additional attributes that make them unique. Everest goals are associated with positive deviance—extraordinarily positive performance. They are associated with Aristotle's goods of first intent, which have inherent value and a sense of calling associated with their pursuit. Everest goals possess an affirmative orientation rather than a problem-solving orientation—the pursuit of the good trumps the mere elimination of a problem. They aim to provide a contribution regardless of personal benefit. And, Everest goals create and foster sustainable positive energy. They require a support system and a process for maintaining focus, but the pursuit of the goal itself is energizing.

6
HOW TO APPLY POSITIVE LEADERSHIP IN ORGANIZATIONS

Practicing positive leadership involves more than the personal pursuit of excellence or the demonstration of individual capabilities. The organizational context must be taken into account, and organizational behavior entails much more complexity than does individual behavior. Organizations have multiple constituencies that must be addressed; processes, routines, and structures that have to be considered; and cultures, embedded values, and traditions that need to be respected. Employee preferences and relationships must be taken into account, and competitors and customers must be acknowledged. Given all these demands, it is helpful to have a framework to help you identify priorities and trade-offs in applying positive leadership practices in organizational settings.

The framework we will use is called the Competing Values Framework. It was developed 30 years ago as my colleagues and I were studying what makes organizations effective. This framework has become among the most utilized in the world to analyze organizational challenges and lead improvement. It highlights the trade-offs and tensions that exist in every high performing organization.

In this chapter, the framework is used to identify four issues that must be dealt with in every organization—focusing on customers, empowering employees, creating new ideas and innovations, and fostering efficiency. We will explore one positive leadership practice associated with each of these four issues.

These practices will help leaders who face criticism that positive leadership is synonymous with easy-going, smiley-faced, touchy-feely practices. Using the Competing Values Framework will expand their leadership repertoire and produce positive results that are not synonymous with mere softness or sweetness.

POSITIVE LEADERSHIP IN ORGANIZATIONS

As pointed out before, there is abundant empirical evidence that practicing positive leadership produces desirable outcomes in organizations. Studies from the Center for Positive Organizations at the University of Michigan demonstrate that practicing positive leadership in organizations across multiple industries—financial services, health care, military organizations, government agencies, transportation, manufacturing, education, airlines, pharmaceuticals, and families—leads to improved performance. Profitability, productivity, quality, innovation, customer loyalty, and employee engagement all improve.[1] One particularly powerful illustration of the effects of positive leadership comes from Jim Mallozzi, a former

CEO and senior executive in the financial services industry. In one business, Jim was charged with leading the merger of two very large financial services organizations.

> We were trying to merge the two cultures together, and in the beginning it was like trying to merge the Red Sox and the Yankees; we had two distinct cultures—one from New England and the other one from the New York/New Jersey area. Both were very strong, very passionate, and very powerful. As you can imagine, trying to put these two cultures together was a challenge.[2]

Over a two-year period, Jim and his colleagues systematically implemented positive leadership practices in the company. They began with senior executive retreats, training and development experiences for leaders across departments and functions, and cascading activities that embedded positive leadership practices among all levels of the merged organization.

> It was a conscious two-year effort that involved not only the senior leadership who led from the front, but virtually everybody in the entire organization needed to be part of it. It was fun to see all the different groups put their own little twist on positive leadership. There were a variety of tools and techniques that we implemented. . . . The primary outcome was the assimilation of the two companies. We kept 95 percent of our clients. Our annual employee satisfaction scores and employee opinion survey results increased. We had less voluntary turnover, and the earnings of the company started going up at about 20 percent per annum on a compound rate. It

was a real success story. In addition, when the president left to take a job in a different company, the culture and the practices actually stayed in place.[3]

In Jim's next assignment, as CEO of another firm, losses amounted to $140 million the year before he arrived and were projected to be $70 million for the current year.

> I harkened back to my previous experience and what I learned about positive leadership. . . . We started with a variety of exercises to show that when you start with the positive, when you ask people to genuinely help you achieve what you're trying to do, fabulous things can happen . . . it really was a case of setting an example in a very public way. . . . As I said, when I took over, the company wasn't doing very well. We had lost a lot of money. Well, sure enough, we went from a $70 million loss to a $20 million profit, and we actually achieved two times our expected business plan. We doubled our profits from what we'd expected. Our employee satisfaction scores went up in nine out of twelve categories.[4]

A FRAMEWORK FOR ORGANIZING POSITIVE PRACTICES

So what was Jim's secret? How did he achieve such extraordinary results in two large, complex financial services organizations? One valuable tool for him was the Competing Values Framework, which helped him organize his priorities and actions.[5]

In brief, the Competing Values Framework is based on two dimensions. Specifically, some organizations and some managers are effective if they are stable, efficient, and predictable. Others are effective if they are flexible, dynamic, and creative. These two competing orientations—stability versus flexibility—represent the vertical axis of the framework. In addition, some organizations and some managers are effective if they create integration, unity, and smoothly flowing internal processes. Others are effective if they are competitive, generate independence, and focus on external constituencies. These two competing orientations—internal focus versus external focus—represent the horizontal axis of the framework. Four quadrants are produced by these two dimensions (see Figure 15).

The quadrants of the Competing Values Framework have been found to be very robust, accurately describing a wide variety of individual phenomena (including cognitive processes, information processing, neurological drives, leadership styles, and managerial competencies) as well as organizational phenomena (including culture, structure, quality processes, human resource management practices, and competitive strategy).[6] We have conducted about three decades of research on this framework, and it is now used by tens of thousands of organizations worldwide. Most important for our purposes is that these quadrants help organize the major practices that positive leaders can implement to achieve positive performance in organizations.

FIGURE 15

The Competing Values Framework

CLAN QUADRANT
Emphasis: Collaboration
Leadership Practice:
Empowering employees

ADHOCRACY QUADRANT
Emphasis: Creativity
Leadership Practice:
Reciprocity network

HIERARCHY QUADRANT
Emphasis: Control
Leadership Practice:
Eliminating inefficiencies

MARKET QUADRANT
Emphasis: Competition
Leadership Practice:
Developing customer loyalty

Source: Cameron and Quinn, 2011; Cameron, Quinn, DeGraff, and Thakor, 2006.

To be effective, leaders must maintain efficient, predictable, and well-oiled organizational processes. This represents the Hierarchy quadrant with its emphasis on maintaining control. Too much emphasis on stability and control, however, creates a frozen bureaucracy, so leaders must also pay attention to the competing quadrant with its emphasis on creativity—the Adhocracy quadrant. Change, flexibility, and dynamic innovation are also important for effective positive leadership. An overemphasis on creativity and change, however, leads to expensive program-of-the-month dynamics.

Similarly, effective leaders must engender teamwork, cohesion, and cooperative interpersonal relationships—a focus of the Clan quadrant, with its emphasis on collaboration. On the other hand, an overemphasis on these dynamics ignores the need for immediate results, fast action, competition, and attention to external customers.[7] The Market quadrant helps balance out the soft approach to leadership with a focus on competition and immediate results. Here, though, an overemphasis on competition leads to an oppressive sweatshop atmosphere. Because of the problems that result from overemphasizing one of the quadrants at the expense of the others, the Competing Values Framework highlights the need to apply positive leadership practices in each quadrant.

One criticism of positive leadership, for example, is that it over-emphasizes soft, touchy-feely, smiley-face, saccharine-sweet, team-focused, cohesive activity. The hard-nosed, competitive, and challenging aspects of leadership are ignored. This criticism is legitimate if positive leadership is limited only to Clan Quadrant practices, but the Competing Values Framework helps remind and guide leaders to be more well-rounded in their implementation.

Not all positive leadership practices can be reliably categorized into one of the four Competing Values Framework quadrants, of course, but many positive practices can be. And this framework can help positive leaders identify which practices are most relevant for their own organizational settings. The framework was one of the key tools used by Jim Mallozzi in guiding his positive leadership turnarounds.

Specifically, Jim organized a change team consisting of positive energizers to disseminate positive leadership practices throughout his organization (see Chapter 3).

They were able to introduce more positive leadership concepts—which in this case was the Competing Values Framework—and it was even more well-received than the initial introduction of positive leadership to the top officers. The team introduced the competing values framework rapidly into our organization. They have now created their own self-sustaining effort in continuing to bring the practices of positive leadership into our organization. It has been fabulous to see.[8]

EXAMPLES OF POSITIVE LEADERSHIP PRACTICES IN EACH QUADRANT

While it is not possible to identify a comprehensive list of positive practices across all four quadrants, of course, Figure 15 highlights one exemplary practice in each quadrant.

Market Quadrant: Customer Loyalty

Every organization has customers—defined as those who receive or are affected by the product or service being delivered. Customers can be internal, that is, members of the organization itself, or external, outside the organization. Most organizations are well aware of the need to satisfy their customers. The American Customer Satisfaction Index is a well-known instrument for identifying the extent to which customers are satisfied with various organizations and industries.[9] Customer satisfaction scores have been found to be a good predictor of company return on investment, net cash flow, and stock returns.[10]

Customer loyalty, however, is different from customer satisfaction. Essentially, loyal customers are those that are unlikely to leave, will repurchase goods and services, and will recommend the product or service to others.[11] Loyal customers' commitment to the organization is much greater than the commitment of merely satisfied customers.

One practical tool for enhancing customer loyalty is based on the Kano model (see Figure 16).[12] This model specifies two dimensions—a satisfaction dimension ("I

FIGURE 16

The Kano Model

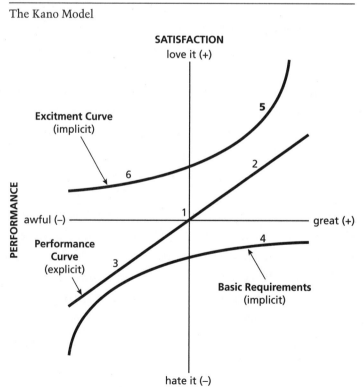

love it" [+] or "I hate it" [–]) and a performance dimension ("Performance is great" [+] or "Performance is awful" [–]). To illustrate, let us assume that you are in the market for a new automobile, and you visit a dealership to purchase the car. You specify for the salesperson the model you want and the features that you prefer—say, four doors, power package, good gas mileage, and black color. If the salesperson shows you this exact car with these precise features—exactly what you request—your position on the Kano model chart is right in the center of the performance curve (point 1). This curve is based on features that the customer asks for directly. In this case, you are perfectly satisfied—not ecstatic and not disappointed—because the car's performance matches your spoken expectations. If, however, you discover that the car handles much better, is quieter, and has a more powerful engine than you expected—that is, the car's performance exceeds your expectations—your position on the performance curve moves up (point 2). You are more satisfied.

If, however, you find that the car has no carpet, no gear shift knob, and no wiper blades, you will probably not want to buy the car. But you would likely never explicitly ask the salesperson for a car with carpet, a gear shift knob, and wiper blades. Those are just basic requirements. If they are not present, dissatisfaction is high (point 3). However, if the salesperson gives you an Elvis Presley rhinestone-studded gear shift knob, it is unlikely to increase your satisfaction. That is, a great deal of money can be spent trying to improve the performance of basic requirements, but satisfaction is not improved at all. There are some things that must be present, but if they are extraordinary, it does not matter (point 4). Improvement in basic requirements has little payoff after they meet essential needs.

On the other hand, if you find that the car has a voice-activated GPS system, a backup camera with an automatic braking feature, a remote entry and start feature, and free service during the 100,000-mile warranty period—that is, it possesses features that you did not expect and did not request, but which address issues that solve problems for you—your position on the Kano model chart is at point 5. This is the excitement curve. It produces customer loyalty, not merely customer satisfaction. If these features are not present, you are not dissatisfied (point 6). But their unexpected presence produces allegiance to the dealership, the likelihood of future purchases, and increased recommendations to others. Companies can expect a 400 percent increase in revenues when they get customers on the excitement curve.[13] The principle is: *Solve a problem for a customer that he or she did not expect to be solved and did not request.* This represents positively deviant performance and produces customer loyalty.

One caveat in the model is that, over time, excitement factors become basic requirements. Customers come to expect the features that at one time were surprises and delights. This means that the challenge of finding ways to surprise and delight customers, to solve their problems, by identifying features on the excitement curve is never finished.

Market Quadrant

Consider your areas of responsibility in your organization. Think of both internal and external customers. Select your key customer for this activity. Identify the value you provide in three areas:

1. Basic curve: value you *must* deliver (implicit)
2. Performance curve: value you *should* deliver (explicit)
3. Excitement curve: value you *could* deliver (implicit)

Take these factors into account:

- What does your customer expect from you?
- What problems does your customer face that neither you nor anyone else is expected to solve?
- What excitement factors could you deliver to engender customer loyalty?

Clan Quadrant: Empowerment

A positive leadership practice associated with the Clan quadrant is the empowerment of employees. It is important to point out that while *empowerment* and *power* are often confused, they are not the same thing. Power always comes from an external source—it can be bestowed on someone—and is defined as the capacity to get someone else to do what you want them to do. Empowerment, on the other, comes from an internal source—it must be personally accepted—and is defined as the capacity to get others to do what they themselves want to do.[14] The leadership challenge, therefore, is to ensure that what others want matches what is best for the organization.

A great deal of research confirms that empowered employees are more productive, more satisfied, and more innovative than unempowered employees.[15] Organizational performance is significantly greater when empowerment scores are high among employees, and neither managers nor organizations can experience long-term, sustained effectiveness without a sense of empowerment.[16]

Based on the research of Gretchen Spreitzer and Aneil Mishra, empowerment is likely to be produced when five factors or dimensions are present.[17] Each of these five dimensions is necessary, so if any one is absent, empowerment will not occur.

The Five Dimensions of Empowerment

Dimension	Explanation
Self-efficacy	A sense of personal competence
Self-determination	A sense of personal choice
Personal consequence	A sense of having impact
Meaning	A sense of value in activity
Trust	A sense of security

Self-efficacy: Empowered people feel confident and competent. They have a sense that they have the skills, abilities, knowledge, and resources to successfully accomplish the tasks with which they are faced, and that they have relationships with others that provide support.

Self-determination: Empowered people sense that they have choice and alternatives. They have discretion and options available so they can pursue what they desire, use the methods of their choice, and therefore they can take responsibility for the outcomes they produce.

Personal consequence: Empowered people are aware of the consequences of their actions. They see the effects of their actions on customers and on broader organizational goals, and they receive feedback on their contribution to those outcomes.

Meaning: Empowered people see the meaningfulness of the activities in which they are engaged. They have a conviction that what they do is attached to a core principle, to something they care about, to something worthy of their time and effort—something that can create a legacy.

Trust: Empowered people have a sense of security. They have confidence that they will hear and can speak the truth, that they will not be harmed or personally maligned, and that they will be treated fairly.

Below are several suggestions for facilitating empowerment across these five dimensions, many of which have emerged from empirical research. Of course, this is not a comprehensive list, and the suggestions are provided here primarily as thought starters. For example, self-efficacy can be fostered by providing personal mastery experiences—breaking apart large tasks and assigning one part at a time, or assigning simple tasks before diffi-cult tasks, or highlighting and celebrating small wins.[18]

Facilitating Empowerment

SELF-EFFICACY (A SENSE OF PERSONAL COMPETENCE)
• Provide personal mastery experiences
• Connect actions to successful outcomes and effects
• Model successful behaviors

SELF-DETERMINATION (A SENSE OF PERSONAL CHOICE)
• Clarify the overriding vision and goals, not actions
• Provide information
• Point out more than one alternative

PERSONAL CONSEQUENCE (A SENSE OF IMPACT)
• Connect with recipients of the outcomes
• Provide resources (time, space, equipment, authority)
• Recognize, encourage, and celebrate successes

MEANING (A SENSE OF VALUE IN THE ACTIVITY)
• Clarify long-term consequences
• Highlight virtuousness and values linked to the activity
• Connect to admired role models and exemplary successes

TRUST (A SENSE OF SECURITY)
• Provide honest feedback using supportive communication
• Offer support for development and growth opportunities
• Exhibit consistency, fairness, and openness

Activity
Clan Quadrant

Answer these two questions: (1) What can I do to enhance my own empowerment? (2) What can I do to help create an empowering environment? The first question relates to your own circumstances at work. The other relates to the way in which you can contribute to others.

Share your ideas with colleagues. Ask your colleagues to add at least one new suggestion to your answers for each of the five dimensions of empowerment.

Adhocracy Quadrant: Generalized Reciprocity

Positive leadership practices that focus on the Adhocracy quadrant are designed, among other things, to enhance innovation and creativity and to uncover unrecognized resources in the organization. One positive practice relies on *generalized reciprocity*.[19] Generalized reciprocity occurs when a person contributes something that is not directly connected to the receipt of something personally beneficial. The contribution occurs because it will be good for someone else.

When Jim Mallozzi had his first meeting as CEO with 2,500 sales personnel in a large auditorium, he asked participants to take out their iPhones and BlackBerrys and text or email one great idea to a special company address for how to get a new client, how to close a sale, or how to keep a customer for life. More than

2,200 ideas were shared, and Mallozzi reported that a number of these ideas were still being actively used fifteen months later.

Generalized reciprocity occurs when one person provides benefit to someone else—such as giving a gift or sharing an idea—without keeping track of its value and without expecting anything in return. The assumption is that the value provided will balance out over time as others provide benefits to their associates.

A positive practice that helps organizations identify new ideas and previously unrecognized resources relies on this principle of generalized reciprocity. Introduced by Wayne Baker, a professor at the University of Michigan, the practice is designed to construct a reciprocity network (see www.humaxnetworks.com).[20] Baker found that constructing reciprocity networks in five different organizations produced more than three-quarters of a million dollars in value and saved almost eight thousand hours.[21]

Reciprocity networks are created among individuals in an organization—even a temporary organization such as a class or a gathering—by having individuals identify needs or requests and then having others in the organization respond to those needs or requests with resources or contacts.

Building a reciprocity network can be done with four steps:

1. Write on a whiteboard or flip chart the names of each of the people in the organization, group, or gathering.

2. Each of those people writes down a specific request, need, or issue with which he or she needs help. These issues may be personal or work-related. The requests must be SMART—that is, they must have the following characteristics:

> S = *Specific*: a resource or resolution to the request must be available
>
> M = *Meaningful*: the request is not trivial or irrelevant but refers to something important
>
> A = *Action-oriented*: there must be action that can be taken in response to the request
>
> R = *Real need*: the request must be tied to a genuine need
>
> T = *Time-bound*: a time frame is given for when a response to the request is needed

Examples of work-related requests might be: "I need to fill a vacancy in the accounting department with a CPA this month," "I need a new IT software system to streamline our inventory control," "I need to become more recognized as a potential leader in my organization," or "I need to determine how to downsize my unit by 15 percent."

The individual verbally describes the request to his or her colleagues and posts it below, or next to, his or her name. An easy way to do this is to write the request on a Post-it note.

3. Each colleague identifies the resources (knowledge, information, expertise, budget, product, emotional

support, and so on) or contacts (someone he or she knows who can provide the resource) in response to as many requests as possible. These contributions are written on a Post-it along with his or her name so that follow-up connections can be made. Each response is posted below the relevant request. Then, in public, each person takes the time to verbally share his or her contributions to the requests for which he or she can add value. Sharing aloud these contributions tends to stimulate the thinking of others who may also realize some additional resource or contribution.

4. After each person has had a chance to explain aloud his or her contributions, provide time for the people who made the requests to connect with each colleague who offered resources or contacts.

An important outcome of this practice is to uncover new ideas and new resources that were previously unknown or unrecognized. Baker found that individuals who offer the most contributions tend to be rated as more competent leaders, more interpersonally effective, and higher performers in their organizations than others.[22] That is, people who are willing to demonstrate generalized reciprocity—to contribute without expecting a personal benefit in return—tend to be more successful as positive leaders.

Activity
Adhocracy Quadrant

In your organization, team, or gathering, or even in your family, follow the steps of the reciprocity network exercise. Ask each member to make a request, offer contributions, and connect with newly uncovered resources.

A Process for Building Reciprocity Networks

1. Make a request (identify a need or specify a problem), post it, and explain it briefly.
2. Determine in what ways you might be able to help with what others have requested. What resources do you possess or know about? How might you add value? Post and explain your contributions.
3. Allow time for requesters and providers of resources and contacts to connect.

Hierarchy Quadrant: Eliminate Inefficiencies

The Hierarchy quadrant, with its emphasis on control, sometimes possesses a negative connotation, since bureaucracy, red tape, and micromanagement are often linked to this quadrant. Positive leaders, however, are cognizant of organizations' need for measurement, accountability, and efficiency, which help balance out the Adhocracy quadrant's emphasis on vision, creativity, new resources, and new ideas.

Although a large number of practices are available for ensuring accountability, efficiency, measurement, and control, only one is briefly discussed here. It emerged from studies of organizational downsizing in which organizations sought to increase efficiency and control by eliminating jobs and headcount.[23] Downsizing is the single most implemented organizational change strategy in the world, but it is frequently unsuccessful in achieving the desired results. Inefficiency, increased costs, and deteriorating quality are often the consequences.[24]

One major reason for these negative results was highlighted by an executive whose firm had experienced several rounds of downsizing:

> The most cost savings in our organization can be generated by improving coordination, collaboration, trust, communication, and information sharing. Most of our costs reside in these soft factors. Yet these costs are not systematically measured. We really have no process for keeping track of, or for managing, our actual costs. We don't even really know what our true costs are given these soft factors. Unless we take a very different approach than we have in the past, our downsizing efforts will again be misplaced and will never really be effective.[25]

Inefficiencies and lack of control in organizations— often called "organizational fat"— frequently remain unmonitored, unmeasured, and even unrecognized. They add costs, create waste, and foster disorganization. Here are a number of examples:

Data Fat: excess programs, unusable information, hard to find data

Idea Fat: suggestions that are never implemented, excessive discussions, dogmatic perspectives

Procedure Fat: excessive audits, documentation, permissions, meetings, paperwork

Career Fat: self-aggrandizement, self-centeredness, lack of teamwork

Belief Fat: uninformed opinions, excess disagreement, recalcitrant positions

Training Fat: unused, irrelevant, or ineffective training; no application or follow-up

Supervision Fat: too many administrators, lack of empowerment, centralized decisions

Time Fat: repetition, redundancy, lack of responsiveness, missed deadlines

Learning Fat: redundant first-time learning, excessive re-learning, off-target learning

Launch Fat: new programs, initiatives, or entrepreneurial activity that are launched but not sustained

Leadership Fat: de-energizing, non-empowering, lack of vision, politicized decisions

Activity
Hierarchy Quadrant

Consider the organization in which you are now working. Identify the major sources of organizational fat. What is not properly controlled? What causes inefficiency and waste? Use the list above, but include other sources particular to your organization. Identify one action that you might take or suggest to trim at least one source of fat.

CONCLUSION

Positive leaders must take into account the specific organizational context in which they find themselves, because practices and tools are not universally applicable in every situation. The organization's customers, processes, routines, employees, and culture all help dictate how effective positive leadership can be practiced. The Competing Value Framework can guide the selection of appropriate positive leadership practices that help address the competing demands in organizations.

7
A BRIEF SUMMARY OF POSITIVE LEADERSHIP PRACTICES

Positive leadership refers to the implementation of multiple positive practices that help individuals and organizations achieve their highest potential, flourish at work, experience elevating energy, and achieve levels of effectiveness difficult to attain otherwise. The practices included in this book have proven to be effective in producing extraordinarily positive results.

Positive leadership is much too rare in organizations because people tend to pay more attention to negative factors than positive factors and because "bad is stronger than good."[1] Crises and difficulties dominate agendas, and organizations are usually in the business of solving problems. Managers' daily tasks tend to focus primarily on addressing challenges and overcoming obstacles. The daily pressures organizations face frequently drive out positive practices.

This is why the practices and activities introduced in this book can be helpful. The activities provide very specific tools that you can implement almost immediately. The practices can enable positive performance and overcome the effects of the negative. Each of these practices is based on empirical evidence and sound theory, and all have been successfully applied in organizations pursuing extraordinarily positive performance.

These practices are based on the four key strategies associated with positive leadership introduced in an earlier book, *Positive Leadership*. They provide practical guidelines for implementing these strategies, as illustrated in Figure 17.

Chapter 2 explains how to create a culture of abundance. This is in contrast to an organization that focuses mainly on solving problems, overcoming crises, or achieving targets and goals. Abundance goes beyond that. Because culture is usually the primary factor that determines whether or not organizational change will be successful, building an organization's culture based on abundance is essential if you are looking for positively deviant results.[2] Here are the guidelines:

Developing a Culture of Abundance

CREATE READINESS

- Provide comparison standards
- Modify language, labels, logos, or symbols

OVERCOME RESISTANCE

- Reduce restraining forces
- Increase driving forces

ARTICULATE A VISION OF ABUNDANCE

- Identify both right-brain and left-brain elements
- Identify a legacy
- Communicate what is interesting

FIGURE 17

Positive Leadership Practices That Lead to Positive Strategies

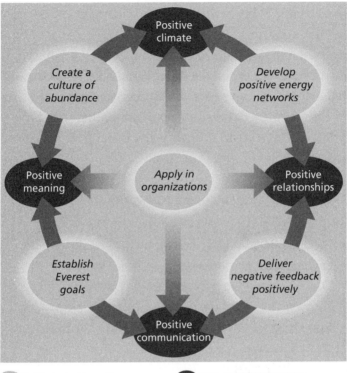

Positive leadership practices   Positive leadership strategies

GENERATE COMMITMENT
- Highlight small wins
- Encourage public commitments

FOSTER SUSTAINABILITY
- Produce metrics, measures, and milestones
- Identify relevant stories

- Foster social support
- Demonstrate personal sacrifice

Chapter 3 shows that positive leadership and positive energy are closely tied together. Positive energy is not an inherent attribute of personality or charisma. It is developed, rather, by demonstrating a set of skills and behaviors that can be learned. By constructing diagrams of the energy networks in your organization, you can see how to utilize positive energy and foster positive performance. Here are some guidelines:

Developing Positive Energy Networks

VALUE-ADDED CONTRIBUTIONS PRACTICE
- Produce positive and developmental feedback for each other
- Distribute it
- Provide time for interpretation
- Encourage public commitments aimed at added contribution

CONTEMPLATIVE PRACTICE
- Engage in a short period of lovingkindness meditation each day
- Keep a gratitude journal

RECREATIONAL WORK
- Incorporate recreational attributes into work
- Structure fun into daily work

POSITIVE ENERGY NETWORKS
- Generate an energy network among your people using statistical mapping

- Generate a bubble chart to identify positive energizers
- Conduct a pulse survey to track energy

Chapter 4 addresses an almost universal challenge of positive leaders: how to give negative or corrective feedback, solve problems, and mitigate conflict and disagreements while maintaining strong, positive relationships. Supportive communication provides guidelines for how to deliver negative feedback, address tensions, and resolve difficult interpersonal problems in ways that enrich and strengthen relationships rather than cause them to deteriorate. Here are the guidelines:

Providing Negative Feedback Positively

POSITIVE-TO-NEGATIVE RATIO

- Make at least three positive statements (and preferably five) for every negative statement
- Ensure honesty and genuineness

CONGRUENCE, NOT INCONGRUENCE

- Ensure that statements are consistent with thoughts and feelings
- Display authenticity and sincerity in statements

DESCRIPTIVE, NOT EVALUATIVE

- Objectively describe the behavior
- Describe consequences and/or feelings
- Make suggestions for acceptable alternatives

PROBLEM ORIENTED, NOT PERSON ORIENTED

- Focus on problems, not personal attributes
- Identify comparison standards, not opinions
- Avoid using "you"

VALIDATING, NOT INVALIDATING
- Avoid superiority, rigidity, indifference, and imperviousness
- Communicate egalitarian, flexible, two-way, and consensus-building statements

Everest goals are different from normal goals. Chapter 5 shows how Everest goals extend beyond common stretch goals by including not just SMART attributes (specific, measurable, aligned, realistic, and time-bound) but also five unique attributes: positive deviance, goods of first intent, affirmative orientation, contribution, and sustainable positive energy. These attributes help elevate the Everest goal beyond mere personal achievement. The guidelines are:

How to Establish and Achieve Everest Goals

ESTABLISHING EVEREST GOALS
   SMART Goal Attributes
- Specific
- Measurable
- Aligned
- Realistic
- Time-bound

   Positive Deviance
- Focus on abundance gaps
- Target extraordinary performance

   Goods of First Intent
- Emphasize inherent value
- Ensure that it is not a means to another end

Affirmative Orientation
- Highlight possibilities, not just probabilities
- Capitalize on strengths

Contribution
- Target providing benefit to others more than personal achievement
- Create unique value

Sustainable Positive Energy
- Focus on what provides intrinsic motivation
- Capitalize on relational energy

ACHIEVING EVEREST GOALS
Specify the Everest Goal
Identify Specific Action Steps
- The more difficult the goal, the more numerous the action steps
- Produce numerous small wins

Measures and Accountability
- Make it more difficult to fail than succeed
- Close loopholes

Effects and Contributions
- Focus on the meaningful contribution
- Identify the inherent value

Chapter 6 helps respond to critics' claims that positive leadership ignores the nard-nosed, competitive, challenging aspects of leadership. It discusses how to apply positive leadership in organizational settings where complex dynamics make it difficult to rely on only one set of practices or activities. The Competing Values Framework is used as an organizing framework for highlighting the trade-offs needed to practice positive leadership in complex circumstances.[3] Here are guidelines for identifying those trade-offs:

*Using the Competing Values Framework to Apply
Positive Leadership in Organizations*

MARKET QUADRANT: CUSTOMER LOYALTY

   Clan Quadrant: Empowering Employees

- Self-efficacy
- Self-determination
- Personal consequence
- Meaning
- Trust

ADHOCRACY QUADRANT: RECIPROCITY NETWORKS

HIERARCHY QUADRANT: ELIMINATING EFFICIENCIES

CONCLUSION

Positive leadership practices can help you begin the process of enabling your organization to achieve extraordinarily successful performance. The suggestions and applications offered here are just a start, but they have proven to be effective in producing positively deviant performance in a variety of settings. Additional tools and positive practices are available, and for additional assistance, books and articles, videos and media, course syllabi and lecture notes, and events and conferences, please see the website of the Center for Positive Organizations at the University of Michigan, www.centerforpos.com.

 # NOTES

Chapter 1 Why Practice Positive Leadership?

1. T. Harada, "Applying Positive Organizational Scholarship in Hayes Lemmertz," video case study, 2012, Center for Positive Organizational Scholarship, University of Michigan.

2. K. S. Cameron and E. Plews, "Positive Leadership in Action: Applications of POS by Jim Mallozzi," *Organizational Dynamics* 41 (2012): 99–105.

3. For a good summary of this research, see K. S. Cameron and G. M. Spreitzer, *The Oxford Handbook of Positive Organizational Scholarship* (New York: Oxford University Press, 2012).

4. For an example, see K. S. Cameron and E. Plews, "Positive Leadership in Action: Applications of POS by Jim Mallozzi," *Organizational Dynamics* 41 (2012): 99–105.

5. For a discussion of the heliotropic effect as applied in organizations, see K. S. Cameron, "Paradox in Positive Organizational Change," *Journal of Applied Behavioral Science* 44 (2008): 7–24.

6. Ibid. See also M. Matlin and D. Stang, *The Pollyanna Principle* (Cambridge, MA: Schenkman, 1978).

7. Several excellent examples of this research are B. L. Fredrickson, *Positivity* (New York: Crown, 2009); B. K. Holzel, J. Carmody, M. Vangel, C. Congeton, S. M. Yerravetti, T. Gard, and S. W. Lazar, "Mindfulness Practice Leads to Increases in Regional Brain Gray Matter Density," *Psychiatry Research: Neuroimaging* 191 (2010): 36–43; Matlin and Stang, *The Pollyanna Principle*; R. McCraty and D. Childre, "The Grateful Heart," in R. A. Emmons and M. E. McCullough, eds., *The Psychology of Gratitude*, 230–55 (New York: Oxford University Press, 2004).

8. S. D. Pressman and S. Cohen, "Positive Emotion Words and Longevity in Famous Deceased Psychologists," *Health Psychology* 31 (2012): 297–305.

9. T. Kraft and S. D. Pressman, "Relationships Between Emotional Word Use in Love Songs and Singer Longevity." Presentation at the International Positive Psychology Association, 2012, Philadelphia, PA.

10. D. A. Snowden, *Aging with Grace: What the Nun Study Teaches Us About Leading Longer, Healthier, and More Meaningful Lives* (New York: Bantam, 2001).

11. R. F. Baumeister, E. Bratslavsky, C. Finkenauer, and K. D. Vohs, "Bad Is Stronger than Good," *Review of General Psychology* 5 (2001): 323–70.

12. Ibid., 323.

13. Studies of the effect of positive leadership practices on organizational performance include K. S. Cameron, D. A. Bright, and A. Caza, "Exploring the Relationships Between Organizational Virtuousness and Performance," *American Behavioral Scientist* 47 (2004): 766–90; K. S. Cameron, C. Mora, T. Leutscher, and M. Calarco, "Effects of Positive Practices on Organizational Effectiveness," *Journal of Applied Behavioral Science* 47 (2011): 266–308; and J. H. Gittell, K S. Cameron, S. Lim, and V. Rivas, "Relationships, Layoffs, and Organizational Resilience," *Journal of Applied Behavioral Science* 42 (2006): 300–328.

14. Gittell et al., "Relationships, Layoffs, and Organizational Resilience," 318.

15. Ibid., 320–28.

16. Cameron et al., "Effects of Positive Practices on Organizational Effectiveness."

Chapter 2 How to Create a Culture of Abundance

The material in this chapter is drawn in part from K. S. Cameron, "Leading Positive Change," in D. A. Whetten and K. S. Cameron, *Developing Management Skills*, 8th ed. (Upper Saddle River, NJ: Prentice Hall, 2011).

1. For a discussion of the importance of organizational culture and a process for managing and changing organizational culture, see K. S. Cameron and R. E. Quinn, *Diagnosing and Changing Organizational Culture* (San Francisco: Jossey-Bass, 2011).

2. See, for example, A. Edmans, "The Link Between Job Satisfaction and Firm Value, with Implications for Corporate Social Responsibility," *Academy of Management Perspectives* 26 (2012): 1–9; K. S. Cameron, C. Mora, T. Leutscher, and M. Calarco, "Effects of Positive Practices on Organizational Effectiveness," *Journal of Applied Behavioral Science* 47 (2011): 266–308; K. S. Cameron and E. Plews, "Positive Leadership in Action: Applications of POS by Jim Mallozzi," *Organizational Dynamics* 41 (2012): 99–105.

3. T. Gold, *Open Your Mind, Open Your Life* (Springfield, IL: Andrews McMeel, 2002).

4. K. S. Cameron and R. E. Quinn, *Diagnosing and Changing Organizational Culture* (San Francisco: Jossey-Bass, 2011).

5. For a sampling of those studies, see K. S. Cameron, *Positive Leadership*, rev. ed. (San Francisco: Berrett-Koehler, 2012); and B. Owens, W. Baker, and K. S. Cameron, "Relational Energy at Work: Establishing Construct, Nomological, and Predictive Validity," working paper, Center for Positive Organizational Scholarship, 2013, University of Michigan.

6. W. G. Bennis and B. Nanus, *Leaders: The Strategies for Taking Charge* (New York: Harper and Row, 1984).

7. K. Lewin, *Field Theory in Social Science* (New York: Harper and Row, 1951).

8. W. G. Bennis, K. D. Benne, and R. Chin, *The Planning of Change* (New York: Holt, Rinehart, and Winston, 1969).

9. L. Kohlberg, *The Philosophy of Moral Development* (New York: Harper and Row, 1981).

10. M. Davis, "That's Interesting!" *Philosophy of the Social Sciences* 1 (1971): 309–44.

11. From the Apple annual reports in the late 1980s.

12. For an excellent discussion of the practical value of small wins from the person who introduced this concept, see K. E. Weick, "Small Wins: Redefining the Scale of Social Problems," *American Psychologist* 39 (1981): 40–49; and K. E. Weick, "Small Wins in Organizational Life," *Dividend* (Winter 1993): 20–24.

13. G. R. Salancik, "Commitment and Control of Organizational Behavior and Belief," in B. M. Staw and G. R. Salancik, eds., *New Directions in Organizational Behavior* (Chicago: St. Clair Press, 1977).

14. For references to several studies see W. Baker, *Achieving Success Through Social Capital* (San Francisco: Jossey-Bass, 2001); and

R. B. Cialdini, *Influence: Science and Practice*, 4th ed. (Boston: Allyn and Bacon, 2001).

15. K. Lewin, *Field Theory in Social Science* (New York: Harper and Row, 1951).

16. For a good discussion of the power of stories in culture change, see J. Martin, *Cultures in Organizations* (New York: Oxford University Press, 1992); and J. Martin, M. Feldman, M. J. Hatch, and S. Sitkin, "The Uniqueness Paradox in Organizational Stories," *Administrative Science Quarterly* 28 (1983): 438–52.

17. For evidence, see J. H. Gittell, K. S. Cameron, S. Lim, and V. Rivas, "Relationships, Layoffs, and Organizational Resilience," *Journal of Applied Behavioral Science* 42 (2006): 300–28; and B. B. Caza and L. P. Milton, "Resilience at Work: Building Capability in the Face of Adversity," in K. S. Cameron and G. M. Spreitzer, eds., *Oxford Handbook of Positive Organizational Scholarship*, 895–908 (New York: Oxford University Press, 2012).

18. For additional models and approaches to culture change, see Cameron and Quinn, *Diagnosing and Changing Organizational Culture*.

Chapter 3 How to Develop Positive Energy Networks

1. For example, see studies summarized in W. Baker, R. Cross, and L. Wooten, "Positive Organizational Network Analysis and Energizing Relationships," in K. S. Cameron, J. E. Dutton, and R. E. Quinn, eds., *Positive Organizational Scholarship: Foundations of a New Discipline*, 328–42 (San Francisco: Berrett-Koehler, 2003); and G. M. Spreitzer, C. F. Lam, and R. W. Quinn, "Human Energy in Organizations," in K. S. Cameron and G. M. Spreitzer, eds., *Oxford Handbook of Positive Organizational Scholarship*, 155–67 (New York: Oxford University Press, 2012).

2. C. G. Brown, *The Energy of Life: The Science of What Makes Our Minds and Bodies Work* (New York: Free Press, 1999).

3. C. P. Alderfer, *Existence, Relatedness, and Growth: Human Needs in Organizational Settings* (New York: Free Press, 1972).

4. C. D. McClelland, *Human Motivation* (New York: Cambridge University Press, 1988).

5. E. A. Locke and G. P. Latham, "Building a Practically Useful Theory of Goal Setting and Task Motivation: A 35-Year Odyssey," *American Psychologist* 57, no. 9 (2002): 705–17.

6. V. Vroom, *Work and Motivation* (New York: Wiley, 1964).

7. L. Festinger, "A Theory of Social Comparison Processes," *Human Relations* 7, no. 2 (1954): 117–40.

8. D. S. DeRue and S. J. Ashford, "Who Will Lead and Who Will Follow? A Social Process of Leadership Identity Construction in Organizations," *Academy of Management Review* 35 (2010): 627–47.

9. W. Baker, R. Cross, and L. Wooten, "Positive Organizational Network Analysis and Energizing Relationships," in K. S. Cameron, J. E. Dutton, and R. E. Quinn, eds., *Positive Organizational Scholarship: Foundations of a New Discipline*, 328–42 (San Francisco: Berrett-Koehler, 2003).

10. B. Owens, W. Baker, and K. S. Cameron, "Relational Energy at Work: Establishing Construct, Nomological, and Predictive Validity," working paper, Center for Positive Organizational Scholarship, 2013, University of Michigan.

11. Ibid.

12. M. S. Cole, H. Bruch, and B. Vogel, "Energy at Work: A Measurement Validation and Linkage to Unit Effectiveness," *Journal of Organizational Behavior* 33 (2011): 445–67.

13. For example, see W. Baker, *Achieving Success Through Social Capital* (San Francisco: Jossey-Bass, 2001).

14. G. M. Spreitzer, C. F. Lam, and R. W. Quinn, "Human Energy in Organizations," in K. S. Cameron and G. M. Spreitzer, eds., *Oxford Handbook of Positive Organizational Scholarship*, 155–67 (New York: Oxford University Press, 2012).

15. See B. L. Fredrickson, M. A. Cohn, K. A. Coffey, J. Pek, and S. M. Finkel, "Open Hearts Build Lives: Positive Emotions, Induced Through Loving Kindness Meditation, Build Consequential Personal Resources," *Journal of Personality and Social Psychology* 95 (2008): 1045–62, and B. E. Kok, K. A. Coffey, M. A. Cohn, L. I. Catalino, T. Vacharkulksemsuk, S. B. Algoe, M. Brantley, and B. L. Fredrickson, "How Positive Emotions Build Physical Health: Perceived Positive Social Connections Account for Upward Spirals Between Positive Emotions and Vagal Tone," working paper, University of North Carolina, 2012, Chapel Hill.

16. B. L. Fredrickson, *Love 2.0* (New York: Hudson Street Press, 2013).

17. B. K. Holzel, J. Carmody, M. Vangel, C. Congeton, S. M. Yerametti, T. Gard, and S. W. Lazar, "Mindfulness Practice Leads to

Increases in Regional Brain Gray Matter Density." *Psychiatry Research: Neuroimaging* 191 (2010): 36–43.

18. See ibid. and S. W. Lazar, C. E. Kerr, R. H. Wasserman, J. R. Gray, D. N. Greve, M. T. Treadway, M. McGarvey, B. T. Quinn, J. A. Dusek, H. Benson, S. L. Rauch, C. I. Moore, and B. Fischl, "Meditation Experience Is Associated with Increased Cortical Thickness," *Neuro Report* 16 (2005): 1893–97.

19. Kok et al., "How Positive Emotions Build Physical Health"; Fredrickson et al., "Open Hearts Build Lives."

20. C. A. Hutcherson, E. M. Seppala, and J. J. Gross, "Loving-Kindness Meditation Increases Social Connectedness," *Emotion* 8 (2008): 720–24.

21. L. E. Sandelands, "The Play of Change," *Journal of Organizational Change Management* 23 (2010): 71–86.

22. C. A. Coonradt, *The Game of Work* (Layton, UT: Gibbs Smith, 2007), 2.

23. Ibid.

24. W. Baker, R. Cross, and L. Wooten, "Positive Organizational Network Analysis and Energizing Relationships," in K. S. Cameron, J. E. Dutton, and R. E. Quinn, eds., *Positive Organizational Scholarship: Foundations of a New Discipline*, 328–42 (San Francisco: Berrett-Koehler, 2003).

Chapter 4 How to Deliver Negative Feedback Positively

This material relies partially on Kim Cameron, "Building Relationships by Communicating Supportively," in D. A. Whetten and K. S. Cameron, *Developing Management Skills*, 8th ed. (Upper Saddle River, NJ: Prentice Hall).

1. For an excellent source, see J. E. Dutton and B. R. Ragins, *Exploring Positive Relationships at Work: Building a Theoretical and Research Foundation* (Mahwah, NJ: Lawrence Erlbaum, 2007).

2. For a review of this literature, see E. D. Heaphy and J. E. Dutton, "Positive Social Interactions and the Human Body at Work: Linking Organizations and Physiology," *Academy of Management Review* 33 (2008): 137–63.

3. Also see J. E. Dutton, *Energizing your Workplace: Building and Sustaining High Quality Relationships at Work* (San Francisco: Jossey-Bass, 2003).

4. An excellent source of this work is J. H. Gittell, "A Theory of Relational Coordination," in K. S. Cameron, J. E. Dutton, and R. E. Quinn, eds., *Positive Organizational Scholarship* (San Francisco: Berrett-Koehler, 2003); see also J. H. Gittell, K. S. Cameron, S. Lim, and V. Rivas, "Relationships, Layoffs, and Organizational Resilience," *Journal of Applied Behavioral Science* 42 (2006): 300–28.

5. M. Losada and E. Heaphy, "The Role of Positivity and Connectivity in the Performance of Business Teams," *American Behavioral Scientist* 47 (2004): 740–65.

6. For additional research, see J. M. Gottman, *What Predicts Divorce: The Relationship Between Marital Processes and Marital Outcomes* (Hillsdale, NJ: Lawrence Erlbaum, 1994); and B. L. Fredrickson, *Positivity* (New York: Crown, 2009).

7. C. W. Rogers, *On Becoming a Person* (Boston: Houghton Mifflin, 1961).

8. J. R. Gibb, "Defensive Communication," *Journal of Communication* 11 (1961): 141–48.

9. Losada and Heaphy, "The Role of Positivity and Connectivity."

10. For excellent research on negotiations, see M. H. Bazerman, *Negotiating Rationally* (New York: Free Press, 1994); and R. Fisher, W. L. Ury, and B. Patton, *Getting to Yes: Negotiating Agreement Without Giving In* (London: Penguin, 2011).

Chapter 5 How to Establish and Achieve Everest Goals

1. For an example of Everest goal achievement, see K. S. Cameron and M. Lavine, *Making the Impossible Possible: Leading Extraordinary Performance—The Rocky Flats Story* (San Francisco: Berrett-Koehler, 2006).

2. An extensive literature exists on goals and goal setting, and among the most interesting are A. Bandura and E. A. Locke, "Negative Self-Efficacy and Goal Effects Revisited," *Journal of Applied Psychology* 88 (2003): 87–99; J. Crocker and A. Canevello, "Creating and Undermining Social Support in Communal Relationships: The Role of Compassionate and Self-Image Goals," *Journal of Personality and Social Psychology* 95 (2008): 555–75; J. S. Lawrence and J. Crocker, "Academic Contingencies of Self-Worth Impair Positively- and Negatively-Stereotyped Students' Performance in Performance-Goal Settings," *Journal of Research in Personality* 43 (2009): 868–74;

L. J. Rawsthorne and A. J. Elliot, "Achievement Goals and Intrinsic Motivation: A Meta-Analytic Review," *Personality and Social Psychological Review* 3 (1999): 326–44; and R. M. Ryan and E. L. Deci, "Self-Determination Theory and the Facilitation of Intrinsic Motivation, Social Development, and Well-Being," *American Psychologist* 55 (2000): 68–78.

3. For an excellent review of the literature on goal setting, see E. A. Locke and G. P. Latham, "New Directions in Goal-Setting Theory," *Current Directions in Psychological Science* 15, no. 5 (2006): 265–68.

4. Ibid.

5. T. T. Mayne, "Negative Affect and Health: The Importance of Being Earnest," *Cognition and Emotion* 13 (1999): 601–35.

6. Cameron and Lavine, *Making the Impossible Possible.*

7. Aristotle, *Metaphysics* XII, 3.

8. Ibid., 4.

9. For a discussion of inherent or intrinsic motivation, see E. L. Deci, R. Koestner, et al., "A Meta-Analytic Review of Experiments Examining the Effects of Extrinsic Rewards on Intrinsic Motivation," *Psychological Bulletin* 125, no. 6 (1999): 627–68.

10. For seminal work on the notion of calling associated with work, see A. Wrzniewski, "Callings," in K. S. Cameron and G. M. Spreitzer, eds., *The Oxford Handbook of Positive Organizational Scholarship*, 45–55 (New York: Oxford University Press, 2012).

11. For a discussion of these kinds of attributes, see R. M. Ryan and E. L. Deci, "On Happiness and Human Potentials: A Review of Research on Hedonic and Eudaemonic Well-Being," *Annual Review of Psychology* 52 (2001): 141–66.

12. J. Crocker, M.-A. Olivier, and N. Nuer, "Self-Image Goals and Compassionate Goals: Costs and Benefits," *Self and Identity* 8 (2009): 251–69.

13. E. L. Deci, *Why We Do What We Do: Understanding Self-Motivation* (New York: Penguin, 1996).

14. E. A. Locke and G. P. Latham, "Building a Practically Useful Theory of Goal Setting and Task Motivation: A 35-Year Odyssey," *American Psychologist* 57, no. 9 (2002): 705–17.

15. For an in-depth summary of this project, see Cameron and Lavine, *Making the Impossible Possible.*

16. Terry Kosdrosky, "Building a Fortune with the Base of the Pyramid: A Q&A with Professors Stuart Hart and Ted London," *Dividend* (Spring 2011): 12.

Chapter 6 How to Apply Positive Leadership in Organizations

1. For examples of these studies, see D. A. Bright, K. S. Cameron, and A. Caza, "The Amplifying and Buffering Effects of Virtuousness in Downsized Organizations," *Journal of Business Ethics* 64 (2006): 249–69; K. S. Cameron, D. A. Bright, and A. Caza, "Exploring the Relationships Between Organizational Virtuousness and Performance," *American Behavioral Scientist* 47 (2004): 766–90; K. S. Cameron and M. Lavine, *Making the Impossible Possible: Leading Extraordinary Performance—The Rocky Flats Story* (San Francisco: Berrett-Koehler, 2006); K. S. Cameron, C. Mora, T. Leutscher, and M. Calarco, "Effects of Positive Practices on Organizational Effectiveness," *Journal of Applied Behavioral Science* 47 (2011): 266–308; and J. H. Gittell, K. S. Cameron, S. Lim, and V. Rivas, "Relationships, Layoffs, and Organizational Resilience," *Journal of Applied Behavioral Science* 42 (2006): 300–28.

2. K. S. Cameron and E. Plews, "Positive Leadership in Action: Applications of POS by Jim Mallozzi," *Organizational Dynamics* 41 (2012): 99.

3. Ibid., 100.

4. Ibid., 102.

5. For in-depth discussions of the Competing Values Framework, its development, and research findings, see K. S. Cameron, R. E. Quinn, J. DeGraff, and A. Thakor, *Competing Values Leadership: Creating Value in Organizations* (Northampton, MA: Edward Elgar, 2006), and also R. E. Quinn and J. Rohrbaugh, "A Special Model of Effectiveness Criteria: Towards a Competing Values Approach to Organizational Analysis," *Management Science* 29 (1981): 363–77.

6. For examples of a variety of applications of models parallel to the Competing Values Framework, see K. S. Cameron and E. Ettington, "The Conceptual Foundations of Organizational Culture," in J. Smart, ed., *Higher Education: Handbook of Theory and Research* (New York: Agathon, 1988); P. R. Lawrence and N. Nohria, *Driven: How Human Nature Shapes Our Choices* (San Francisco: Jossey-Bass, 2002); I. I. Mitroff, *Stakeholders of the Organizational Mind* (San Francisco: Jossey-Bass, 1983); and K. Wilber, *A Theory of Everything: An Integral Vision of Business, Politics, Science, and Spirituality* (Boston: Shambhala Books, 2001).

7. For criticisms of positive leadership and the focus on positivity in organizations, see S. Fineman, "On Being Positive: Concerns

and Counterpoints," *Academy of Management Review* 31, no. 2 (2006): 270–91; J. M. George, "Book Review of *Positive Organizational Scholarship: Foundations of a New Discipline*," *Administrative Science Quarterly* 49 (2004): 325–30; and B. Ehrenreich, *Bright-Sided: How Positive Thinking Is Undermining America* (New York: Henry Holt, 2009).

8. Cameron and Plews, "Positive Leadership in Action," 103.

9. This work is best described by the founder of this index in C. Fornell, R. T. Rust, and M. G. Dekimpe, "The Effect of Customer Satisfaction on Consumer Spending Growth," *Journal of Marketing Research* 47 (2010): 28–35.

10. C. Fornell, S. Mithas, F. V. Morgeson III, and M. S. Krishnan, "Customer Satisfaction and Stock Prices: High Returns, Low Risk," *Journal of Marketing* 70, no. 1 (2006): 3–14.

11. Examples from this literature include F. Reichheld, *The Loyalty Effect* (Boston: Harvard Business School Press, 1996); and K. Storbacka, T. Strandvik, and C. Gronroos, "Managing Customer Relationships for Profit," *International Journal of Service Industry Management* 5 (1994): 21–28.

12. N. Kano, N. Seraku, F. Takahashi, and S. Tsuji, "Attractive Quality and Must-Be Quality" (in Japanese), *Journal of the Japanese Society for Quality Control* 14, no. 2 (1984): 39–48.

13. J. L. Stasser, W. E. Heskett, and L. A. Schlesinger, *The Service Profit Chain* (New York: Free Press, 1997).

14. K. S. Cameron, "Empowering and Delegating," in D. A. Whetten and K. S. Cameron, *Developing Management Skills*, 8th ed. (Upper Saddle River, NJ: Prentice Hall, 2011).

15. See, for example, D. B. Greenberger and S. Stasser, "The Role of Situational and Dispositional Factors in the Enhancement of Personal Control in Organizations," *Research in Organizational Behavior* 13 (1991): 111–45; and G. M. Spreitzer, "When Organizations Dare: The Dynamics of Individual Empowerment in the Workplace," Ph.D. dissertation, 1992, University of Michigan.

16. J. A. Conger and R. N. Kanungo, "The Empowerment Process," *Academy of Management Review* 13 (1988): 471–82; R. E. Quinn and G. M. Spreitzer, "The Road to Empowerment: Seven Questions Every Leader Should Consider," *Organizational Dynamics* 25 (1997): 37–49.

17. Spreitzer, "When Organizations Dare"; A. K. Mishra, "Organizational Response to Crisis: The Role of Mutual Trust and Top

Management Teams," Ph.D. dissertation, 1992, University of Michigan.

18. For an excellent discussion of self-efficacy, personal mastery experiences, and social learning theory, see A. Bandura, *Social Foundations of Thought and Action: A Social Cognitive Theory* (Englewood Cliffs, NJ: Prentice Hall, 1986).

19. Excellent discussions of generalized reciprocity and its applicability to organizations are W. Baker, "A Dual Model of Reciprocity in Organizations," in K. S. Cameron and G. M. Spreitzer, eds., *The Oxford Handbook of Positive Organizational Scholarship* (New York: Oxford University Press, 2012), and W. Baker, "Making Pipes, Using Pipes: How Tie Initiation, Reciprocity, and Positive Emotions Create New Organizational Social Capital," in S. P. Borgatti, D. J. Brass, D. S. Halgin, G. Labianca, and A. Mehra, eds., *Research in the Sociology of Organizations, Volume on Contemporary Perspectives on Organizational Social Network Analysis* (forthcoming).

20. Reciprocity networks are also called Reciprocity Rings. See www.humaxnetworks.com.

21. Baker, "Making Pipes, Using Pipes."

22. Baker, "A Dual Model of Reciprocity in Organizations."

23. For studies of organizational downsizing, see K. S. Cameron, "Strategies for Successful Organizational Downsizing," *Human Resource Management Journal* 33 (1994): 89–112; K. S. Cameron, "Strategic Organizational Downsizing: An Extreme Case," *Research in Organizational Behavior* 20 (1998): 185–229; K. S. Cameron, S. J. Freeman, and A. K. Mishra, "Best Practices in White-Collar Downsizing: Managing Contradictions," *Academy of Management Executives* 5 (1991): 57–73; and C. L. Cooper, A. Pandey, and J. C. Quick, *Downsizing: Is Less Still More?* (Cambridge: Cambridge University Press, 2012).

24. Cameron, "Strategic Organizational Downsizing: An Extreme Case."

25. Cameron et al., "Best Practices in White-Collar Downsizing."

Chapter 7 A Brief Summary of Positive Leadership Practices

1. R. F. Baumeister, E. Bratslavsky, C. Finkenauer, and K. D. Vohs, "Bad Is Stronger Than Good," *Review of General Psychology* 5 (2001): 323–70.

2. K. S. Cameron and R. E. Quinn, *Diagnosing and Changing Organizational Culture* (San Francisco: Jossey-Bass, 2011).

3. K. S. Cameron, R. E. Quinn, J. DeGraff, and A. Thakor, *Competing Values Leadership: Creating Value in Organizations* (Northampton, MA: Edward Elgar, 2006).

PRACTICING POSITIVE LEADERSHIP SELF-ASSESSMENT

The Practicing Positive Leadership Self-Assessment (http://www.bkconnection.com/positive-leadership-sa) is an instrument designed to diagnose the extent to which you are demonstrating positive leadership practices and implementing positive strategies. The questions are organized into sections so that you can be aware of which strategy and which practice is being assessed. The Berrett-Koehler website will provide comparison data so that you can see how you compare with others who have completed the instrument.

☀ REFERENCES

Alderfer, C. P. *Existence, Relatedness, and Growth: Human Needs in Organizational Settings*. New York: Free Press, 1972.

Aristotle. *Metaphysics*.

Baker, W. *Achieving Success Through Social Capital*. San Francisco: Jossey-Bass, 2001.

———. "A Dual Model of Reciprocity in Organizations." In K. S. Cameron and G. M. Spreitzer, eds., *Oxford Handbook of Positive Organizational Scholarship*. New York: Oxford University Press, 2012.

———. "Making Pipes, Using Pipes: How Tie Initiation, Reciprocity, and Positive Emotions Create New Organizational Social Capital." In S. P. Borgatti, D. J. Brass, D. S. Halgin, G. Labianca, and A. Mehra, eds., *Research in the Sociology of Organizations, Volume on Contemporary Perspectives on Organizational Social Network Analysis* (forthcoming).

Baker, W., R. Cross, and L. Wooten. "Positive Organizational Network Analysis and Energizing Relationships." In K. S. Cameron, J. E. Dutton, and R. E. Quinn, eds., *Positive Organizational Scholarship: Foundations of a New Discipline*, pp. 328–42. San Francisco: Berrett-Koehler, 2003.

Bandura, A. *Social Foundations of Thought and Action: A Social Cognitive Theory*. Englewood Cliffs, NJ: Prentice Hall, 1986.

Bandura, A., and E. A. Locke. "Negative Self-Efficacy and Goal Effects Revisited." *Journal of Applied Psychology* 88 (2003): 87–99.

Baumeister, R. F., E. Bratslavsky, C. Finkenauer, and K. D. Vohs. "Bad Is Stronger than Good." *Review of General Psychology* 5 (2001): 323–70.

Bazerman, M. H. *Negotiating Rationally.* New York: Free Press, 1994.

Bennis, W. G., K. D. Benne, and R. Chin. *The Planning of Change.* New York: Holt, Rinehart, and Winston, 1969.

Bennis, W. G., and B. Nanus. *Leaders: The Strategies for Taking Charge.* New York: Harper and Row, 1984.

Bright, D. A., K. S. Cameron, and A. Caza. "The Amplifying and Buffering Effects of Virtuousness in Downsized Organizations." *Journal of Business Ethics* 64 (2006): 249–69.

Brown, C. G. *The Energy of Life: The Science of What Makes Our Minds and Bodies Work.* New York: Free Press, 1999.

Cameron, K. S. "Leading Positive Change." In D. A. Whetten and K. S. Cameron, *Developing Management Skills,* 8th ed. Upper Saddle River, NJ: Prentice Hall, 2011.

———. "Paradox in Positive Organizational Change." *Journal of Applied Behavioral Science* 44 (2008): 7–24.

———. *Positive Leadership.* Rev. ed. San Francisco: Berrett-Koehler, 2012.

———. "Strategic Organizational Downsizing: An Extreme Case." *Research in Organizational Behavior* 20 (1998): 185–229.

———. "Strategies for Successful Organizational Downsizing." *Human Resource Management Journal* 33 (1994): 89–112.

Cameron, K. S., D. A. Bright, and A. Caza. "Exploring the Relationships Between Organizational Virtuousness and Performance." *American Behavioral Scientist* 47 (2004): 766–90.

Cameron, K. S., and E. Ettington. "The Conceptual Foundations of Organizational Culture." In J. Smart, ed., *Higher Education: Handbook of Theory and Research.* New York: Agathon, 1988.

Cameron, K. S., S. J. Freeman, and A. K. Mishra. "Best Practices in White-Collar Downsizing: Managing Contradictions." *Academy of Management Executives* 5 (1991): 57–73.

Cameron, K. S., and M. Lavine. *Making the Impossible Possible: Leading Extraordinary Performance—The Rocky Flats Story.* San Francisco: Berrett-Koehler, 2006.

Cameron, K. S., C. Mora, T. Leutscher, and M. Calarco. "Effects of Positive Practices on Organizational Effectiveness." *Journal of Applied Behavioral Science* 47 (2011): 266–308.

Cameron, K. S., and E. Plews. "Positive Leadership in Action: Applications of POS by Jim Mallozzi." *Organizational Dynamics* 41 (2012): 99–105.

Cameron, K. S., and R. E. Quinn. *Diagnosing and Changing Organizational Culture.* San Francisco: Jossey-Bass, 2011.

Cameron, K. S., R. E. Quinn, J. DeGraff, and A. Thakor. *Competing Values Leadership: Creating Value in Organizations.* Northampton, MA: Edward Elgar, 2006.

Cameron, K. S., and G. M. Spreitzer. *The Oxford Handbook of Positive Organizational Scholarship.* New York: Oxford University Press, 2012.

Cameron, K. S., and B. Winn. "Virtuousness in Organizations." In K. S. Cameron and G. M. Spreitzer, eds., *The Oxford Handbook of Positive Organizational Scholarship,* pp. 231–43. New York: Oxford University Press, 2012.

Caza, B. B., and L. P. Milton. "Resilience at Work: Building Capability in the Face of Adversity." In K. S. Cameron and G. M. Spreitzer, eds., *The Oxford Handbook of Positive Organizational Scholarship,* pp. 895–908. New York: Oxford University Press, 2012.

Cialdini, R. B. *Influence: Science and Practice.* 4th ed. Boston: Allyn and Bacon, 2001.

Cole, M. S., H. Bruch, and B. Vogel. "Energy at Work: A Measurement Validation and Linkage to Unit Effectiveness." *Journal of Organizational Behavior* 33 (2011): 445–67.

Conger, J. A., and R. N. Kanungo. "The Empowerment Process." *Academy of Management Review* 13 (1988): 471–82.

Coonradt, C. A. *The Game of Work.* Layton, UT: Gibbs Smith Press, 2007.

Cooper, C. L., A. Pandey, and J. C. Quick. *Downsizing: Is Less Still More?* Cambridge: Cambridge University Press, 2012.

Crocker, J., and A. Canevello. "Creating and Undermining Social Support in Communal Relationships: The Role of Compassionate and Self-Image Goals." *Journal of Personality and Social Psychology* 95 (2008): 555–75.

Crocker, J., M.-A. Olivier, and N. Nuer. "Self-Image Goals and Compassionate Goals: Costs and Benefits." *Self and Identity* 8 (2009): 251–69.

Davis, M. "That's Interesting!" *Philosophy of the Social Sciences* 1 (1971): 309–44.

Deci, E. L. *Why We Do What We Do: Understanding Self-Motivation.* New York: Penguin, 1996.

Deci, E. L., R. Koestner, et al. "A Meta-Analytic Review of Experiments Examining the Effects of Extrinsic Rewards on Intrinsic Motivation." *Psychological Bulletin* 125, no. 6 (1999): 627–68.

DeRue, D. S., and S. J. Ashford. "Who Will Lead and Who Will Follow? A Social Process of Leadership Identity Construction in Organizations." *Academy of Management Review* 35 (2010): 627–47.

Dutton, J. E. *Energizing your Workplace: Building and Sustaining High Quality Relationships at Work.* San Francisco: Jossey-Bass, 2003.

Dutton, J. E., and B. R. Ragins. *Exploring Positive Relationships at Work: Building a Theoretical and Research Foundation.* Mahwah, NJ: Lawrence Erlbaum, 2007.

Edmans, A. "The Link Between Job Satisfaction and Firm Value, with Implications for Corporate Social Responsibility." *Academy of Management Perspectives* 26 (2012): 1–9.

Ehrenreich, B. *Bright-Sided: How Positive Thinking Is Undermining America.* New York: Henry Holt, 2009.

Festinger, L. "A Theory of Social Comparison Processes." *Human Relations* 7, no. 2 (1954): 117–40.

Fineman, S. "On Being Positive: Concerns and Counterpoints." *Academy of Management Review* 31, no. 2 (2006): 270–91.

Fisher, R., W. L. Ury, and B. Patton. *Getting to Yes: Negotiating Agreement Without Giving In.* London: Penguin, 2011.

Fornell, C., S. Mithas, F. V. Morgeson III, and M. S. Krishnan. "Customer Satisfaction and Stock Prices: High Returns, Low Risk." *Journal of Marketing* 70, no. 1 (2006): 3–14.

Fornell, C., R. T. Rust, and M. G. Dekimpe. "The Effect of Customer Satisfaction on Consumer Spending Growth." *Journal of Marketing Research* 47, no. 1 (2010): 28–35.

Fredrickson, B. L. *Love 2.0.* New York: Hudson Street Press, 2013.

———. *Positivity*. New York: Crown Books, 2009.

Fredrickson, B. L., M. A. Cohn, K. A. Coffey, J. Pek, and S. M. Finkel. "Open Hearts Build Lives: Positive Emotions, Induced Through Loving Kindness Meditation, Build Consequential Personal Resources." *Journal of Personality and Social Psychology* 95 (2008): 1045–62.

George, J. M. "Book Review of *Positive Organizational Scholarship: Foundations of a New Discipline*." *Administrative Science Quarterly* 49 (2004): 325–30.

Gibb, J. R. "Defensive Communication." *Journal of Communication* 11 (1961): 141–48.

Gittell, J. H. "A Theory of Relational Coordination." In K. S. Cameron, J. E. Dutton, and R. E. Quinn, eds., *Positive Organizational Scholarship*. San Francisco: Berrett-Koehler, 2003.

Gittell, J. H., K. S. Cameron, S. Lim, and V. Rivas. "Relationships, Layoffs, and Organizational Resilience." *Journal of Applied Behavioral Science* 42 (2006): 300–28.

Gold, T. *Open Your Mind, Open Your Life*. Springfield, IL: Andrews McMeel, 2002.

Gottman, J. M. 1994. *What Predicts Divorce: The Relationship Between Marital Processes and Marital Outcomes*. Hillsdale, NJ: Erlbaum.

Greenberger, D. B., and S. Stasser. "The Role of Situational and Dispositional Factors in the Enhancement of Personal Control in Organizations." *Research in Organizational Behavior* 13 (1991): 111–45.

Harada, T. "Applying Positive Organizational Scholarship in Hayes Lemmetrz." Video case study. Center for Positive Organizational Scholarship, University of Michigan, 2012.

Heaphy, E. D., and J. E. Dutton. "Positive Social Interactions and the Human Body at Work: Linking Organizations and Physiology." *Academy of Management Review* 33 (2008): 137–63.

Heskett, J. L., W. E. Stasser, and L. A. Schlesinger. *The Service Profit Chain*. New York: Free Press, 1997.

Holzel, B. K., J. Carmody, M. Vangel, C. Congeton, S. M. Yerrametti, T. Gard, and S. W. Lazar. "Mindfulness Practice Leads to Increases in Regional Brain Gray Matter Density." *Psychiatry Research: Neuroimaging* 191 (2010): 36–43.

Hutcherson, C. A., E. M. Seppala, and J. J. Gross. "Loving-Kindness Meditation Increases Social Connectedness." *Emotion* 8 (2008): 720–24.

Kano, N., N. Seraku, F. Takahashi, and S. Tsuji. "Attractive Quality and Must-Be Quality" (in Japanese). *Journal of the Japanese Society for Quality Control* 14, no. 2 (1984): 39–48.

Kohlberg, L. *The Philosophy of Moral Development.* New York: Harper and Row, 1981.

Kok, B. E., K. A. Coffey, M. A. Cohn, L. I. Catalino, T. Vacharkulksemsuk, S. B. Algoe, M. Brantley, and B. L. Fredrickson. "How Positive Emotions Build Physical Health: Perceived Positive Social Connections Account for Upward Spirals Between Positive Emotions and Vagal Tone." Working paper, University of North Carolina, Chapel Hill, 2012.

Lawrence, J. S., and J. Crocker. "Academic Contingencies of Self-Worth Impair Positively- and Negatively-Stereotyped Students' Performance in Performance-Goal Settings." *Journal of Research in Personality* 43 (2009): 868–74.

Lawrence, P. R., and N. Nohria. *Driven: How Human Nature Shapes Our Choices.* San Francisco: Jossey-Bass, 2002.

Lazar, S. W., C. E. Kerr, R. H. Wasserman, J. R. Gray, D. N. Greve, M. T. Treadway, M. McGarvey, B. T. Quinn, J. A. Dusek, H. Benson, S. L. Rauch, C. I. Moore, and B. Fischl. "Meditation Experience Is Associated with Increased Cortical Thickness." *Neuro Report* 16 (2005): 1893–97.

Lewin, K. *Field Theory in Social Science.* New York: Harper and Row, 1951.

———. *Resolving Social Conflicts and Field Theory in Social Science.* Washington, DC: American Psychological Association, 1997.

Locke, E. A., and G. P. Latham. "Building a Practically Useful Theory of Goal Setting and Task Motivation: A 35-Year Odyssey." *American Psychologist* 57, no. 9 (2002): 705–17.

———. "New Directions in Goal-Setting Theory." *Current Directions in Psychological Science* 15, no. 5 (2006): 265–68.

Lopez, S., and S. D. Pressman. *The 25 Great Myths of Happiness.* Thousand Oaks, CA: Sage, 2012.

Losada, M., and E. Heaphy. "The Role of Positivity and Connectivity in the Performance of Business Teams." *American Behavioral Scientist* 47 (2004): 740–65.

Martin, J. *Cultures in Organizations.* New York: Oxford University Press, 1992.

Martin, J., M. Feldman, M. J. Hatch, and S. Sitkin. "The Uniqueness Paradox in Organizational Stories." *Administrative Science Quarterly* 28 (1983): 438–52.

Matlin, M., and D. Stang. *Pollyanna Principle.* Cambridge, MA: Schenkman, 1978.

Mayne, T. T. "Negative Affect and Health: The Importance of Being Earnest." *Cognition and Emotion* 13 (1999): 601–35.

McClelland, C. D. *Human Motivation.* New York: Cambridge University Press, 1988.

McCraty, R., and D. Childre. "The Grateful Heart." In R. A. Emmons and M. E. McCullough, eds., *The Psychology of Gratitude*, 230–55. New York: Oxford University Press, 2004.

Mishra, A. K. "Organizational Response to Crisis: The Role of Mutual Trust and Top Management Teams." Ph.D. dissertation, University of Michigan, 1992.

Mitroff, I. I. *Stakeholders of the Organizational Mind.* San Francisco: Jossey-Bass, 1983.

Owens, B., W. Baker, and K. S. Cameron. "Relational Energy at Work: Establishing Construct, Nomological, and Predictive Validity." Working paper, Center for Positive Organizational Scholarship, University of Michigan, 2013.

Pressman, S. D., and S. Cohen. "Positive Emotion Words and Longevity in Famous Deceased Psychologists." *Health Psychology* 31 (2012): 297–305.

Putnam, R. *Bowling Alone.* New York: Simon and Schuster, 2013.

Quinn, R. E., and J. Rohrbaugh. "A Special Model of Effectiveness Criteria: Towards a Competing Values Approach to Organizational Analysis." *Management Science* 29 (1981): 363–77.

Quinn, R. E., and G. M. Spreitzer. "The Road to Empowerment: Seven Questions Every Leader Should Consider." *Organizational Dynamics* 25 (1997): 37–49.

Rawsthorne, L. J., and A. J. Elliot. 1999. "Achievement Goals and Intrinsic Motivation: A Meta-analytic Review." *Personality and Social Psychological Review* 3 (1997): 326–44.

Reichheld, F. *The Loyalty Effect*. Boston: Harvard Business School Press, 1996.

Rogers, C. W. *On Becoming a Person*. Boston: Houghton Mifflin, 1961.

Ryan, R. M., and E. L. Deci. "On Happiness and Human Potentials: A Review of Research on Hedonic and Eudaemonic Well-Being." *Annual Review of Psychology* 52 (2001): 141–66.

———. "Self-Determination Theory and the Facilitation of Intrinsic Motivation, Social Development, and Well-Being." *American Psychologist* 55 (2000): 68–78.

Salancik, G. R. "Commitment and Control of Organizational Behavior and Belief." In B. M. Staw and G. R. Salancik, eds., *New Directions in Organizational Behavior*. Chicago: St. Clair Press, 1977.

Sandelands, L. E. "The Play of Change." *Journal of Organizational Change Management* 23 (2010): 71–86.

Schein, E. H. *Organizational Culture and Leadership*. San Francisco: Jossey-Bass, 2010.

Snowden, D. A. *Aging with Grace: What the Nun Study Teaches Us About Leading Longer, Healthier, and More Meaningful Lives*. New York: Bantam Books, 2001.

Spreitzer, G. M. "When Organizations Dare: The Dynamics of Individual Empowerment in the Workplace." Ph.D. dissertation, University of Michigan, 1992.

Spreitzer, G. M., C. F. Lam, and R. W. Quinn. "Human Energy in Organizations." In K. S. Cameron and G. M. Spreitzer, eds., *The Oxford Handbook of Positive Organizational Scholarship*, 155–67. New York: Oxford University Press, 2012.

Stasser, J. L., W. E. Heskett, and L. A. Schlesinger. *The Service Profit Chain*. New York: Free Press, 1997.

Storbacka, K., T. Strandvik, and C. Gronroos. "Managing Customer Relationships for Profit." *International Journal of Service Industry Management* 5 (1994): 21–28.

Vroom, V. *Work and Motivation*. New York: Wiley, 1964.

Weick, K. E. "Small Wins: Redefining the Scale of Social Problems." *American Psychologist* 39 (1981): 40–49.

———. "Small Wins in Organizational Life." *Dividend* (Winter 1993): 20–24.

Wilber, K. *A Theory of Everything: An Integral Vision of Business, Politics, Science, and Spirituality.* Boston: Shambhala, 2001.

Wrzniewski, A. "Callings." In K. S. Cameron and G. M. Spreitzer, eds., *The Oxford Handbook of Positive Organizational Scholarship*, 45–55. New York: Oxford University Press, 2012.

INDEX

☀ ABOUT THE AUTHOR

**Kim Cameron** is the William Russell Kelly Professor of Management and Organizations in the Ross School of Business and Professor of Higher Education in the School of Education at the University of Michigan. He currently serves as associate dean in the Ross School of Business at the University of Michigan and has served as dean of the Weatherhead School of Management at Case Western Reserve University, as associate dean in the Marriott School of Management at Brigham Young University, and as a department chair at the University of Michigan. He also currently serves as a Fellow in the Wheatley Institution at Brigham Young University.

Cameron is one of the cofounders of the Center for Positive Organizational Scholarship at the University of Michigan—a research center focused on the investigation of positively deviant performance, virtuousness, strengths, and practices in organizations that lead to thriving and extraordinary outcomes. He received B.S. and M.S. degrees from Brigham Young University and M.A. and Ph.D. degrees from Yale University. His research on organizational virtuousness, effectiveness, quality culture, downsizing, and the development of leadership skills has been published in more than 120 academic articles and 14 scholarly books.

Cameron is married to the former Melinda Cummings and has seven children.

Also by Kim Cameron
Positive Leadership
Strategies for Extraordinary Performance, Second Edition

Positive Leadership explores in depth the strategies needed to reach beyond ordinary success and achieve extraordinary effectiveness, spectacular results, and "positively deviant performance." Citing a wide range of research in organizational behavior, medical science, and psychology as well as real-world examples, Cameron shows that to achieve exceptional success, leaders must emphasize strengths rather than simply focus on weaknesses; foster virtuous actions such as compassion, gratitude, and forgiveness; encourage contribution goals in addition to achievement goals; and enable meaningfulness in work. This second edition features updated research findings and new ideas for implementing positive leadership.

Paperback, 176 pages, ISBN 978-1-60994-566-4
PDF ebook, ISBN 978-1-60994-567-1

BK° Berrett–Koehler Publishers, Inc.
San Francisco, *www.bkconnection.com*   **800.929.2929**

Edited with Jane E. Dutton and Robert E. Quinn

Positive Organizational Scholarship

Foundations of a New Discipline

Featuring contributions by internationally renowned scholars and authors, this groundbreaking book focuses on the dynamics in organizations that lead to the development of human strength; foster resiliency in employees; make healing, restoration, and reconciliation possible; and cultivate extraordinary individual and organizational performance.

Hardcover, 480 pages, ISBN 978-1-57675-232-6
PDF ebook, ISBN 978-1-57675-966-0

With Marc Lavine

Making the Impossible Possible

Leading Extraordinary Performance—the Rocky Flats Story

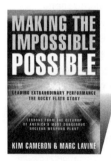

Experts estimated that cleaning up and closing the Rocky Flats nuclear weapons plant would take 70 years and $36 billion—but the project was completed 60 years ahead of schedule and $30 billion under budget. This book explains how other organizations can apply the same methods to achieve breakthrough levels of performance.

Paperback, 296 pages, ISBN 978-1-57675-390-3
PDF ebook, ISBN 978-1-60509-707-7

BK Berrett–Koehler Publishers, Inc.
San Francisco, *www.bkconnection.com*

800.929.2929

Berrett–Koehler
Publishers

Berrett-Koehler is an independent publisher dedicated to an ambitious mission: *Creating a World That Works for All*.

We believe that to truly create a better world, action is needed at all levels—individual, organizational, and societal. At the individual level, our publications help people align their lives with their values and with their aspirations for a better world. At the organizational level, our publications promote progressive leadership and management practices, socially responsible approaches to business, and humane and effective organizations. At the societal level, our publications advance social and economic justice, shared prosperity, sustainability, and new solutions to national and global issues.

A major theme of our publications is "Opening Up New Space." Berrett-Koehler titles challenge conventional thinking, introduce new ideas, and foster positive change. Their common quest is changing the underlying beliefs, mindsets, institutions, and structures that keep generating the same cycles of problems, no matter who our leaders are or what improvement programs we adopt.

We strive to practice what we preach—to operate our publishing company in line with the ideas in our books. At the core of our approach is stewardship, which we define as a deep sense of responsibility to administer the company for the benefit of all of our "stakeholder" groups: authors, customers, employees, investors, service providers, and the communities and environment around us.

We are grateful to the thousands of readers, authors, and other friends of the company who consider themselves to be part of the "BK Community." We hope that you, too, will join us in our mission.

A BK Business Book

This book is part of our BK Business series. BK Business titles pioneer new and progressive leadership and management practices in all types of public, private, and nonprofit organizations. They promote socially responsible approaches to business, innovative organizational change methods, and more humane and effective organizations.

Berrett–Koehler
Publishers

A community dedicated to creating
a world that works for all

Visit Our Website: www.bkconnection.com

Read book excerpts, see author videos and Internet movies, read
our authors' blogs, join discussion groups, download book apps, find
out about the BK Affiliate Network, browse subject-area libraries of
books, get special discounts, and more!

Subscribe to Our Free E-Newsletter, the *BK Communiqué*

Be the first to hear about new publications, special discount offers,
exclusive articles, news about bestsellers, and more! Get on the list
for our free e-newsletter by going to **www.bkconnection.com**.

Get Quantity Discounts

Berrett-Koehler books are available at quantity discounts for orders
of ten or more copies. Please call us toll-free at (800) 929-2929 or
email us at bkp.orders@aidcvt.com.

Join the BK Community

BKcommunity.com is a virtual meeting place where people from
around the world can engage with kindred spirits to create a world
that works for all. **BKcommunity.com** members may create their own
profiles, blog, start and participate in forums and discussion groups,
post photos and videos, answer surveys, announce and register for
upcoming events, and chat with others online in real time. Please join
the conversation!

MIX
From responsible
sources
FSC® C113845

Certified

Corporation
bcorporation.net